PAULIST BIBLE STUDY PROGRAM

Jesus and the Gospels

LEADER'S MANUAL

Workbook by	Kate Dooley, O.P. and Anne Dalton
Video Scripts by	Anthony Marinelli
Prayers by	Rea McDonnell, S.S.N.D.

PAULIST PRESS

New York/Mahwah

Acknowledgements

Faith Sharing Principles are reprinted from RENEW, copyright © 1987 by the Roman Catholic Archdiocese of Newark, New Jersey. Used by permission.

Published by Paulist Press
997 Macarthur Blvd.
Mahwah, New Jersey 07430

Printed and Bound in the United States of America.

TABLE OF CONTENTS

Dear Friends,

It is a pleasure to present our new Paulist Bible Study Program. The Paulist Bible Study Program is designed to help adults understand the Bible in the light of contemporary biblical scholarship and to use the Bible as a source of prayer, reflection and action. It relates the study of the Bible to the liturgy, to the church, and to our daily lives. Those who long to know more about the Bible, based on the authentic Catholic tradition and the most responsible and best biblical scholarship, have a rich experience awaiting them.

Kevin A. Lynch, C.S.P.
Publisher

GENERAL INTRODUCTION

What Is the Paulist Bible Study Program?

The Paulist Bible Study Program brings together the best of contemporary biblical scholarship with the challenge of personal growth in faith. It provides adults with a coordinated approach to studying the Bible which at the same time calls them to personalize the new insights they gain through prayer and sharing with other members of their group.

Bible study is more than Bible reading. It is the discovery of our roots, of the questions we hold in common with our ancestors in faith. It is learning about the world of the Bible, its history, its geography, and its culture. It is also learning to pray with the Bible. That is why the Paulist Bible Study Program incorporates faith sharing, video, prayer, and journal reflection into every session.

The Paulist Bible Study Program begins with a broad overview of the Bible in four units of eight weeks each. There are two units on the Old Testament and two units on the New Testament. The first unit on the Old Testament, *Israel Becomes a People,* introduces participants to the study of the Old Testament and covers the books of Genesis and Exodus. The second unit, *Prophets and Kings,* covers the period from the formation of the monarchy through the Exile. For the New Testament, the first unit, *Jesus and the Gospels,* treats the life and ministry of Jesus and the formation of the Gospel traditions. The second unit, *Paul, Missionary to the Gentiles,* focuses on the life of Paul and his letters.

These units provide the basis for on-going study in the future. Future units will cover additional books or groups of books on the Old and New Testaments.

The Methods of the Program

The Paulist Bible Study Program employs a twofold method of biblical interpretation. The first method could be called the ecclesial method. The ecclesial method interprets the Bible in the context of both the individual's and the church's experience. Each individual who comes to the Bible brings along his or her experience. This experience provides the invaluable context for understanding the Scriptures. The Paulist Bible Study Program seeks to employ the findings of contemporary research on adult education to help participants reflect on and interpret their experience in the light of the Scriptures. This personal context of experience is complemented by the communal context as well. That is why the study of the Bible must also be rooted in the ongoing experience of the church. In every age the church has sought to apply the words of Scripture to its own time and circumstances.

The Bible comes from the church. First received by the people of Israel, and then by the ancient Christian communities, these texts have been judged to be the sacred, inspired word of God by those original communities and by every generation thereafter. Thus, the church must continue to interpret the Scriptures in new ways as its understanding of God's word grows in time. Just as the Spirit of God guided the writers of the Bible and the ancient communities who received their words, so too the Spirit continues to guide the church as it interprets the Scriptures today.

The second method which the Paulist Bible Study Program employs is the historical-critical method. This approach seeks to recover the original meaning of the words written for people of another time and culture. It builds on the insights of ancient history and ancient literary styles that have been proposed by scholars over the last three centuries. The Catholic Church was at first cautious about accepting this method because it developed in a manner that did not always refer to the Bible as a book of faith or a book of the church. However, in 1947, after much reflection, Pope Pius XII issued the encyclical letter *Divino Afflante Spiritu.* This letter summoned Catholic scholars to use the best of this modern scholarship to unlock the history of the biblical texts and to enrich our knowledge of how it expressed its meaning according to the thought patterns of biblical times. Today Catholic scholars, along with scholars of other Christian and Jewish traditions, employ the insights of historians, translators, and archaeologists to recover and convey the original meaning of the Scriptures for contemporary believers.

Who Can Participate in the Paulist Bible Study Program?

The program is designed for adults who want to learn more about the meaning of the Bible and to share their insights with others. Parish-based adult groups, ministry formation groups, small Christian communities, and campus ministry groups will all find this program helpful. One need not have done any previous study of the Bible in order to participate. However, it does require that participants make a commitment to come to each of the sessions and to participate in them. This means that they will need to do the preparatory reading and reflection prior to each session and that they will be open to participating in a communal style of learning: working collaboratively, sharing their questions and insights, and praying together.

It will be important for you, as the Program Leader, to inform participants of the kind of commitment which is necessary. This can be done through whatever publicity you prepare for the program, as well as through your personal contact with prospective participants in the program.

Who Can Be a Leader in the Program?

Anyone having a basic foundation in understanding the Bible according to the methods outlined above can serve as a leader. This Leader's Manual contains all of the information necessary to lead the program. The leader need not be a biblical expert, but should be comfortable in talking about the Bible and in facilitating a group of adults. In addition to the biblical background provided by this manual, there is also a section on adult learning for the leader to use.

It is suggested that there be one Program Leader who is responsible for the planning and implementation of the program. If there is a large number of participants, additional leaders will be necessary. A rule of thumb would be to have one leader for every ten participants. These leaders would facilitate the process in the small groups and would thus need a copy of this manual as well.

Resources for the Program

The Bible: First and most important is the Bible itself. There is no substitute for the actual reading of the Bible and so each week participants will be asked to read some part of the Bible. The recommended translation is the *New American Bible.* At times there are references to the text and the notes in this version. The *Catholic Study Bible,* which uses the *New American Bible* text, is one of the recommended resources for leaders as well as participants.

Companion Texts: As a companion to the reading of the Bible, the program uses these two books: *Reading the Old Testament* by Lawrence Boadt, C.S.P. and *Reading the New Testament* by Pheme Perkins.

Workbook: The Workbooks are a key part of the Paulist Bible Study Program. With the Bible and the companion text, the Workbook forms the third component of the program. For each unit of study there is a Workbook which helps the participant focus on the key passages in the Bible and the companion text. It also provides the basis for the weekly group meeting at which participants review what they have read at home, share their insights, and pray together.

Leader's Manual: For each unit of study there is also a comprehensive Leader's Manual. Besides containing a wealth of background material, it provides complete notes for the Program Leader. There is one Leader's Manual for each unit in the program. These books enable anyone with a basic foundation in the Bible to implement the program and guide a group along its way.

Additional Resources: At the end of each session you will find a number of suggestions for the participant to do additional reading of the Scriptures as well as of other resource books. At times a map exercise is also provided. A listing of the resources recommended for the particular unit is found in the introduction to that unit.

Further Reading: This section is also found at the end of each session, but only in the Leader's Manual. It provides suggestions for additional background reading for the leader, drawn from the *New Jerome Biblical Commentary* as well as other sources. Once again, a listing of the resources recommended for the particular unit is found in the introduction to that unit.

Adult Religious Education

Adult religious education is at the center of the church's ministry. As Pope John Paul II said, "Catechesis for adults is, indeed, the principal form of catechesis, since it is directed to those who have the greatest responsibilities and the ability to live the Christian message in its fullness" (*Catechesi Tradendi,* 43). This focus is repeated in *Sharing the Light of Faith: National Catechetical Directory for Catholics in the United States:* "While aiming to enrich the faith life of individuals at their particular stages of development, every form of catechesis is oriented in some way to the catechesis of adults" (*Sharing the Light of Faith,* 32). The Paulist Bible Study Program is based on this vision of adult religious education and on sound principles of adult learning.

What is adult religious education? In seeking to clarify its meaning, James J. DeBoy distinguishes between *adult learning, adult education,* and *schooling.*[1] For adults, learning is an ongoing process which occurs in a wide variety of ways, both planned and unplanned. Schooling, on the other hand, is structured and comprehensive. All adults have had experience with school. The quality of that experience and the images and emotions that linger from it will, to a large degree, shape the attitudes of adults about further formal educational experiences. Adult education seeks to provide structured learning opportunities for adults. It combines both adult education and schooling, but in a way that expands the model that many adults have of schooling.

What then is adult *religious* education? DeBoy offers this definition: "Adult religious education is the planned effort to provide opportunities to enable adults to awaken and deepen their knowledge, understanding and daily living of their faith."[2] The *General Catechetical Directory* echoes this theme when it notes that the aim of adult religious education is to help adults attain a faith that is living, conscious and active (*General Catechetical Directory,* 17).

In 1985 the U.S. Catholic Conference Department of Education issued a document entitled *Serving Life and Faith: Adult Religious Education and the American Catholic Community.* This document highlights adult religious education as a ministry.

> Adult religious education is a major function of the church's ministry of the word. Sharing the same overarching goals as other functions of that ministry, such as preaching and evangelization, it seeks to do its part by helping adults attain a knowledge and wisdom that matures faith and inspires love (*Serving Life and Faith,* 27).

As a ministry of the word, adult religious education sees learning as a response to God's self-revelation which is rooted in the Scriptures and the church's tradition, and focused on the life and experience of those who learn.

Neil Parent highlights the importance of this experiential dimension:
> While adult religious education does entail passing on the church's rich tradition, it also includes a much broader and dynamic range of activities, including interpreting lived experience in the light of the gospel, helping to solve major challenges in Christian life, and sharing personal faith stories and gifts with one another. Adult religious education is often a voyage of discovery rather than a trip to a known destination. Thus the participants frequently become teachers to one another, drawing upon their own experiences of faith and insights into the gospels.[3]

The Goals of Adult Religious Education

Serving Life and Faith articulates three particular goals of adult religious education which form a helpful backdrop for the Paulist Bible Study Program.

> First, adult religious education is directed at helping individuals and communities understand and live the gospels to the fullest extent possible. Second, adult religious education helps prepare believers to exercise a prophetic voice in today's world, to focus the light of the gospel on the issues of our time. Third, adult religious education is an important means for helping adults share their faith with the next generation (*Serving Life and Faith,* 34-36).

These three objectives could well be applied to the Paulist Bible Study Program. In the context of small groups, it focuses directly on the gospels and thus helps individuals and communities understand and live them. It focuses on the prophetic voice of Jesus and the prophets, encouraging participants to reflect on their message in light of their own experience and contemporary society. And it provides participants with a basic biblical knowledge which equips them to share their faith with the next generation, either as parents or through some other ministry within the church.

The Paulist Bible Study Program has two broad goals: to help adults read and understand the Bible in light of contemporary biblical scholarship; and to foster a biblical spirituality. Developing an understanding of the Bible in light of recent biblical scholarship will enable adults to understand the relationship between the Bible and the findings of contemporary science, history, and archaeology. Understanding the origins of the various books of the Bible within ancient Jewish and Christian communities will enable them to see the Bible as the church's book and to interpret it in light of the church's life and tradition. A greater knowledge of the Bible will foster a heightened awareness of the centrality of the Bible in Christian life.

The development of a biblical spirituality means that adults will learn to pray with the Bible and to appreciate it more within the context of the Eucharist and other liturgical celebrations. A biblical spirituality will help adults reflect on their own experience and recognize God's presence and action within it. Finally, it will help adults appreciate the prophetic challenge that the Bible poses to us and, hopefully, to respond to that challenge. These are among the many general goals of the program. Certainly each parish or community, as well as each participant, should reflect on the goals they bring to this study of the Bible at the outset. And at the conclusion of each unit, they might well reflect on the experience to see what goals have been met, and to what extent they have grown through the experience.

The Qualities of Adult Learners

The Paulist Bible Study Program seeks to accomplish these goals by paying special attention to the qualities of adult learners. Malcolm Knowles has identified the following basic qualities of adult learners:
- The adult learner is a self-directed person who can make his or her own decisions and determine his or her own needs.
- The experience of the adult learner is a rich resource for learning, both for oneself and for others.
- Readiness for adult learning usually develops out of one's problems or tasks in life. An adult's approach to learning situations is specific, centered on the needs he or she has. Thus, adult learners expect to be able to apply what they learn almost immediately to real life.
- Motivation to learn arises from internal curiosity or desire to solve a problem or accomplish a task, not from coercion of any kind.[4]

The Paulist Bible Study Program seeks to incorporate these principles in the following ways:
- It encourages adults to set their own goals and to work toward achieving them.
- It draws on their experience as a resource for learning and invites them to share their insights with others.
- It connects the study of the Bible with life issues and thus opens up the Bible as a resource for facing the challenges and difficulties of life.
- It places adults in a group of their peers where they might share their prayers, questions, and insights and thus learn from one another.

The Components of Each Session

The program seeks to incorporate these principles into each session. Here is a listing of the components of each session with some general suggestions on how you can facilitate the process of adult learning:

Opening Prayer (5 minutes)
Participants begin each session by placing themselves and their group in God's presence, and asking for the guidance of the Holy Spirit during the upcoming session. Invite various members of the group to take turns leading both the opening and the closing prayers.

Review of Contents (25 minutes)
This section gives participants the opportunity to express what they have learned and to learn from the insights of others. At this time, you should encourage participants to raise any questions they might have that are not covered in the Workbook. While you are not expected to have all the answers, you may be able to suggest ways that participants can find the answer to a particular question.

Video (20 minutes)
The video is designed to enrich participants' learning by providing the visual dimension of what they are studying. This will sometimes include photographs of places, objects, and people, and at other times artistic representations. Before viewing the program, direct the participants to look at the highlight questions and jot down the answers as they watch. Afterwards, allow a brief period of time for them to raise any questions or make comments.

Learning Activity (25 minutes)
During this segment, participants work with one another in an exercise to further integrate the meaning of the Scripture they have read and to apply it to their lives. The role of the leader during this segment is to insure that participants understand the task, to facilitate the process of completing it, and to help the groups to share their learning with each other.

Faith Sharing (25 minutes)
Here participants will share together the insights they have gained through prayer and study, and the impact of these insights on their faith. The Workbooks provide questions and suggestions to facilitate this process. Again, the leader's role is to encourage and to enable. The following faith-sharing principles, borrowed from RENEW, should be kept in mind. (These can also be found in the introduction to the Workbook.)

- The entire faith-sharing process is seen as prayer, i.e., listening to the word of God as broken by others' experience.
- Constant attention to respect, honesty and openness for each person will assist the group's growth.
- Each person shares on the level where he or she feels comfortable.
- Silence is a vital part of the total process of faith sharing. Participants are given time to reflect before any sharing begins, and a period of comfortable silence might occur between individual sharings.
- Persons are encouraged to wait to share a second time until others who wish to do so have contributed.
- The entire group is responsible for participating and faith sharing.
- Confidentiality is essential, allowing each person to share honestly.
- Reaching beyond the group in action and response is essential for the growth of individuals, the group, and the church.

Closing Prayer (10 minutes)
Having shared their faith together, participants conclude with a brief period of prayer which often includes singing, praying, and listening to the word of God. If there are various roles or parts to be shared among the group, be sure to invite members to prepare them in advance.

Journaling
For each session, one or more ideas for journal keeping is suggested. Encourage participants to keep a journal, either to do these exercises or simply to write their own reflections.

Additional Resources
Each week, the Workbook refers to a number of sources for further reading and study. You may wish to encourage participants to purchase these resources or you may want to buy them to create a program resource library. See the order form for additional information.

Nine Principles of Adult Religious Education

In concluding this brief introduction to adult religious education and the Paulist Bible Study Program, we offer nine principles of adult religious education, as formulated by James DeBoy, for the leader in this program to keep in mind.

1. Adults learn best when they are treated with respect, as self-directing persons.

2. Adults learn best when the learning situation is related to their past experiences.

3. Adults learn best when they have participated in the planning of the learning activity and set their own goals.

4. Adults learn best when they are physically comfortable and can socialize with those in the learning group.

5. Adults learn best when they are with their peers, freely learning in groups.

6. Adults learn best when there are opportunities for a variety of learning activities.

7. Adults learn best in a problem-centered situation, when a question needs resolving or a task needs doing.

8. Adults learn best when they can see progress, immediate results, and some rewards for the time they put into learning.

9. Adults learn best when they evaluate themselves.[5]

The Format of This Book

For the convenience of the leaders, this book contains the text of both the Leader's Manual and the Workbook. The text which is indented and in larger type is the text found only in the Workbook. The smaller type, which is at the left margin, indicates what is found only in the Leader's Manual.

Notes

1. James J. DeBoy, Jr., *Getting Started in Adult Religious Education* (Ramsey, New Jersey: Paulist Press, 1979), 5.

2. *Ibid.,* 8.

3. Neil Parent, "The Challenges Facing Religious Education Today," *New Catholic World,* 230 (September/October 1987): 237-238.

4. Malcolm Knowles, *The Modern Practice of Adult Education,* rev. ed. (Chicago: Follett, 1981), 43-45.

5. DeBoy, 75-79.

Introduction to the Workbook

Welcome to the Paulist Bible Study Program and to this first unit on the New Testament.

In this unit you will be introduced to the study of the New Testament and to the gospels of Matthew, Mark and Luke. This Workbook will serve as a reading guide to the Bible and to your companion text *Reading the New Testament* by Pheme Perkins. Each week it will point out what passages of the Bible you should read and what parts of the companion text are focused on these passages.

The Bible in the Life of the Church

The emergence of popular interest in the Bible among Catholics stems from the Second Vatican Council. Along with the new emphasis on the Scriptures during the Eucharist and other sacramental celebrations, the Council called upon all members of the church to grow in their knowledge and love of the Bible:

> Just as the life of the church grows through persistent participation in the eucharistic mystery, so we may hope for a new surge of spiritual vitality from intensified veneration for God's word (*Decree on Revelation,* 26).

The vision of the central place of the Scriptures which the Council set forth is becoming more and more a reality.

> The church has always venerated the divine Scriptures just as she venerates the body of the Lord, since from the table of both the word of God and of the body of Christ she unceasingly receives and offers to the faithful the bread of life, especially in the sacred liturgy. She has always regarded the Scriptures together with sacred tradition as the supreme rule of faith, and will ever do so. *Decree on Revelation,* 21).

Our hope is that this program will be yet another resource which will take the process of integrating Scripture into the life of the Church one step further.

Jesus' Own Bible Study Model

In 1986, Archbishop Roger Mahoney of Los Angeles issued a pastoral letter entitled "The Bible in the Life of the Church." One part of the letter reflects on Jesus' own approach to teaching the Scriptures to his disciples as he walked with two of them on the road to Emmaus (Luke 24:13-35). Archbishop Mahoney's reflections on this passage are a fitting introduction to our study of the Bible.

> The two disciples are on their way from Jerusalem to Emmaus when Jesus—his appearance hidden—joins them. He responds to their bewilderment by "interpreting for them every passage of Scripture which referred to him." This was the most clear example of Jesus sharing the Scriptures that we find in the gospels. For our own Bible study to be beneficial, then, we too must

open our hearts and lives to allow Jesus to unlock the meaning of his message for us.

But two additional elements in the Emmaus journey are also required to validate our own experience of the Scriptures. First, our Scripture study must lead towards, center around, and flow from the Eucharist—the Mass. It was only in "the breaking of the bread" that the full meaning of Jesus' explanations became clear to the two men journeying to Emmaus. As Catholics, we too must always focus our Bible studies in and through the Eucharist. And secondly, we must be guided in our Scripture studies through "Simon Peter—the church." Recall that the two men returned in haste to Jerusalem where they were greeted with: "The Lord has been raised! It is true! He has appeared to Simon." This validation by Peter—by the church—is essential to our authentic understanding of the word of God.

The Importance of Commitment

What are your goals for your participation in this program? As you begin, take a few moments to reflect upon your goals and jot them down. These may involve gaining some knowledge, but don't omit other possible gains such as growing in your spirituality or prayer life, building community within your parish. Any goal worth achieving requires commitment. During this program you are invited to make a commitment to grow in your understanding and appreciation of the Bible. All commitments require time. In this case, you are committing yourself to be present at the eight sessions and to participate in the learning process. This will require the most precious of commodities: time.

What follows is a description of the various steps you should take to prepare for and to follow-up on a meeting. Only you can determine how much time you have to spend on these steps. Not everything needs to be done now. Hopefully, the Paulist Bible Study Program will provide you with the resources to continue your own study well after a particular unit ends.

In addition to a time commitment, you are making a commitment to the other participants in your group. You bring unique gifts and experience to this study of the Bible that will enrich your co-learners. The steps below offer some tips on how you can both share your own insights and enable others to share theirs.

Preparing for the Meeting

Each week you will be meeting with others to reflect on the Scriptures and the parts of the companion text. Before you engage in the exercises in this book, follow the steps outlined for each session in the section called Preparation.

1. Prayerfully read the appointed Bible passages. Here is a simple way to do that:

2. Read the assigned portion of the companion text. You may want to read a little bit each day to coordinate with your prayerful reading of the Bible. Many find it helpful to mark the text for key parts or to jot down questions that may arise during a reading.

3. Read the Focus and Review of Contents before the meeting. If you have time, try to work on responses to the review questions. Your companion text also has review questions after each chapter which will be helpful.

During the Meeting

Each session is designed to last two hours. Here are the steps for each session and some suggestions on how to make use of them.

Opening Prayer (5 minutes)

Place yourself and your group in God's presence, asking for the guidance of the Holy Spirit during the upcoming session.

Review of Contents (25 minutes)

This section gives you the opportunity to express what you have learned and to learn from the insights of others. If you have questions other than those raised in the review, bring them up at this time. While your Program Leader cannot be expected to have all the answers, he or she may be able to help you find an answer to your question.

Video (20 minutes)

The video is designed to enrich your learning by providing the visual dimension of what you are studying. Before viewing the program, look at the highlight questions. Jot down the answers as you watch the program. Afterwards, there is a brief time for your to raise questions or make a comment.

Learning Activity (25 minutes)

During this segment, you will work with others in an exercise to further integrate the meaning of the Scripture you have read and to apply it to your life.

Faith Sharing (25 minutes)

The following suggestions, borrowed from RENEW, are helpful guidelines for faith sharing:

- The entire faith-sharing process is seen as prayer, i.e., listening to the word of God as broken by others' experience.
- Constant attention to respect, honesty and openness for each person will assist the group's growth.
- Each person shares on the level where he/she feels comfortable.
- Silence is a vital part of the total process of faith sharing. Participants are given time to reflect before any sharing begins, and a period of comfortable silence might occur between individual sharings.
- Persons are encouraged to wait to share a second time until others who wish to do so have contributed.
- The entire group is responsible for participating and faith sharing.
- Confidentiality is essential, allowing each person to share honestly.
- Reaching beyond the group in action and response is essential for the growth of individuals, the group and the church.

Closing Prayer (10 minutes)

Having shared our faith together, we conclude with prayer. Join in the spirit of the prayer service by singing, praying, and listening to the word of God.

After the Meeting

Journaling
For each session, one or more journal ideas are suggested. You may wish to keep a journal either to do these exercises, or simply to write your own reflections.

Additional Resources
Each week a number of sources are referred to for further reading and study. Your parish may have purchased these books for a parish resource library or you may obtain them from Paulist Press. Your program leader has further information. You may wish to consult these sources for continued study after the unit ends.

Additional Resources

Atlas of the Bible Lands, rev.ed. Edited by Harry Thomas Frank. Maplewood, NJ: Hammond, 1990.

Catholic Study Bible. Edited by Donald Senior. New York: Oxford University Press, 1990.

Responses to 101 Questions on the Bible. Raymond E. Brown, S.S. Mahwah, NJ: Paulist Press, 1990.

Understanding the Gospels. Anthony Marinelli. Mahwah, NJ: Paulist Press, 1988.

Further Reading

The Four Gospels and the Jesus Tradition. John F. O'Grady. Mahwah, NJ: Paulist Press, 1989.

Jesus and the Evangelists. Philip A. Cunningham. Mahwah, NJ: Paulist Press, 1988.

The New Jerome Biblical Commentary. Edited by Raymond E. Brown, S.S., Joseph A. Fitzmeyer, S.J., and Roland E. Murphy, O.Carm. Englewood Cliffs, NJ: Prentice Hall, 1990.

1. What is the New Testament?

General Goals:
— To present a general overview of the New Testament.
— To help participants become familiar with the arrangement, types of writing and general content of the books.
— To reflect upon the place of the Bible in their lives and in the Church today.

FOCUS

We each bring our own personal level of understanding to the study of the New Testament. In this session we will get an overview of the New Testament books and look at the different types of writing found there. We will also explore the meaning of the Scriptures for our lives today.

OPENING PRAYER

Time: 5 minutes

Preparation
Explain to the group that we will begin each week with a short period of prayer. Ask them if they are familiar with the refrain from "Grant to us, O Lord" by Lucien Deiss. If they are, practice it once with them. If not, use the spoken refrain. For this first session, the leader might do the reading.

Song Refrain:
''Grant to us, O Lord'' by Lucien Deiss

or

Spoken Antiphon:
Open our hearts, Holy Spirit, to hear and rejoice in your word.

Reading
A reading from the prophet Jeremiah (31:31-34)

The days are coming, says the Lord, when I will make a new covenant with my people. . . . This is the new testament I will make with you. I will place my word within you and write it in your hearts. I will be your God and you will be my people. All from the least to the greatest will know me, says the Lord. (Paraphrased from Jeremiah 31:31-34).

Song refrain or spoken antiphon

Prayer

Leader:
Let us pray: (Pause)
We are thirsty and we come to you, our God; hungry, and eager to delight in rich food. We want to listen to you that we might have life. We await your word which accomplishes all your desires in us. Come, Word of God!

Song refrain or spoken antiphon

GETTING STARTED

Objective: To help participants become familiar with the program and to acquaint them with the books of the New Testament.

Time: 25 minutes

1. Introduce yourself and, depending on the size of the group, ask the participants to introduce themselves to the whole group or to those sitting near them.

2. Distribute the Workbooks and the text, *Reading the New Testament.* Explain how these are used in the program.
Give a brief presentation of the purpose and format of the Paulist Bible Study Program.

3. Emphasize that there is no competition in a group such as this. The only goal is that people participate in whatever way they can and gain whatever they can. The first session is an introduction to the New Testament in general and to the various books that make it up. This session will raise questions that will form the basis of future study. Assure the group that what is presented in this session will be taken up again in other ways.

> The New Testament has twenty seven books:
>> Four gospels grouped together at the beginning
>> The Acts of the Apostles
>> Thirteen letters, either written by Paul or attributed to him
>>> Paul's letters have a set form:
>>> Greeting
>>> Short prayer
>>> Teaching addressing some problem within the community
>>> Exhortation to live a Christian way of life
>>> Farewell and short blessing
>> Epistle to the Hebrews
>> The seven letters attributed to the apostles
>> The Book of Revelation

4. Ask the group to look at the table of contents for their New Testament. Give a brief overview of the contents of the books as follows, referring them to pages 2-8 of their companion texts as well.

The New Testament has twenty-seven books.

Four gospels grouped together at the beginning. The gospels of Matthew, Mark, and Luke are similar in structure, content, and wording. They are thus called "synoptic" gospels, or gospels having a common view of Jesus. The gospel of John paints a very different picture of Jesus.

The Acts of the Apostles, which is also written by St. Luke and considered the second part of Luke's gospel. It tells the story of the early Church from the Ascension of Jesus to Paul's journey to Rome.

Thirteen letters, either written by Paul or attributed to him. These letters are not arranged chronologically, but are placed in two categories: letters written to churches, letters written to individuals. Within those two categories, the letters are then arranged according to length, with the longest coming first. Paul's letters have a set form:
>Greeting
>Short prayer
>Teaching addressing some problem within the community
>Exhortation to live a Christian way of life
>Farewell and short blessing

Epistle to the Hebrews, which is no longer attributed to Paul and is not a letter. Rather, it is a sermon exhorting these Jewish Christians to remain firm in their faith.

Seven letters attributed to the apostles, usually called catholic epistles. Catholic, in this context, means general; that is, they are not addressed to specific churches or individuals.

The Book of Revelation, symbolic visions about the end of the world.

LEARNING ACTIVITY

Objective: To review the stages of tradition through which the teaching and life of Jesus have come to us.

Time: 25 minutes

1. Ask the group to choose one of the following statements and then to pair off with another participant and to spend a few moments discussing why they chose a particular item.

Put a check next to the statement which comes closest to describing your understanding of the gospels.

_____ 1. The gospels are biographies of all that Jesus did and said when he was on earth.

_____ 2. The gospels are written records of the preaching of the disciples about Jesus in the light of the resurrection. They take into account the mind set, the concerns, and the culture of the listeners.

_____ 3. The gospels are narratives about the words and actions of Jesus and what they mean for people today.

_____ 4. The gospels are part of a cultural inheritance and have importance because they have shaped Western thought and values.

2. Reassemble the group and ask volunteers to offer the statement they chose and to explain why. After group members have offered their reasons for particular choices, it may be helpful to comment on each of the four statements along these lines:

1. While the gospels do record the life and work of Jesus, they are not biographies in our sense of the term. A biography attempts to give a complete account of a person's whole life. The gospels are more selective in what they tell of Jesus' life. After the story of Jesus' birth, they relate little of his life until the beginning of his public ministry. Sometimes they differ in their chronologies or in other details.

2. As a reflection of the original Christian communities, the gospels are written in light of faith in the resurrection as well as in light of the culture and needs of the original communities. In addition, this

5

statement could be expanded to include the ongoing significance of the gospels for the faith of the Church today.

3. This statement aptly notes the contemporary significance of the gospels for the Church, but does not stress the significance of the original setting of the gospels in interpreting them today.

4. The impact of the gospels on Western civilization has been enormous and continues today. However, they cannot be viewed by believers only in this context. Here you may want to add the material from Perkins on the Bible as a "classic," cf. pp. 9-10.

3. Point out that the gospels went through stages of formation. It may also be helpful to summarize the three stages of tradition by which the gospels were formed.

— *The Life of Jesus:* Christ chose certain disciples who followed him from the beginning, who had seen his works and heard his words and thus were qualified to become witnesses of his life and teaching.

— *The Preaching of the Apostles:* They gave witness to Jesus, proclaiming first and foremost the death and resurrection of the Lord and faithfully recounting his life and works. In their preaching they took the circumstances of their hearers into account. Because the disciples had experienced Christ's resurrection and exaltation, they were able to hand on this fuller understanding to their listeners. Just as on the road to Emmaus Jesus had interpreted the Old Testament and his own words to his disciples, now they were able to interpret his words and deeds to their hearers. They used various forms of communication: catechesis, stories, testimonies, hymns, doxologies, prayers, and any other ways of speaking and writing that were found in the Scriptures or used by the people of that time.

— *The written form of the gospels:* The instruction was handed on orally at first and then written down. The sacred authors selected those aspects out of all the material received that would best meet the needs of their particular community and the attainment of their own purposes. The finished gospels we have today probably went through different written stages before reaching their present final form.

BREAK

(10 minutes)

VIDEO

Objective: To introduce the participants to the study of the New Testament, to the variety of books in the New Testament, and to the tools biblical scholars use to understand it.

Time: 20 minutes

An introduction to the books and study of the New Testament.

As you view the video, please make note of the following:

1. What are the four kinds of criticism described in the program?

1. _____

2. _____

3. _____

4. _____

2. What are the three stages of the formation of the gospels?

1. _____

2. _____

3. _____

Video Outline

An introduction to the books and study of the New Testament

1. The centrality of the New Testament for our faith

2. The twofold aim of the program: study and prayerful openness to the word

3. Four tools for studying the New Testament
   a. Historical Criticism: The attempt to understand the written word in light of all the various influences of the culture it comes from
   b. Literary Criticism: The study of the many different literary genres or styles of writing found in the New Testament
      - Epistles: to particular churches
        to the church at large
      - Gospels: The three stages of gospel formation
        preaching of Jesus
        proclamation of the early Church
        the written forms of the gospels
      - Religious History: The Acts of the Apostles
      - Apocalyptic Literature: The Book of Revelation
   c. Form Criticism: The study of the origins of the written word in earlier traditions
   d. Redaction Criticism: An attempt to understand the influence of the final writer on the composition

FAITH SHARING

Objective: To relate the gospel to the lives of the participants and to begin to teach a way of prayer and reflection on the Scriptures.

Time: 25 minutes

Introduce this segment of the program by explaining that at this time we try to appropriate personally the meaning of what we have learned and appreciate its significance for our daily lives. Our aim is to share our own thoughts and feelings and to listen to what others offer. If someone expresses a thought or feeling different from your own, simply listen and try to understand it. Do not comment on the other's statement, but when your turn comes, share your own feelings and ideas.

1. How is Scripture a part of your daily life?

1. If the group is large, break it into smaller groups of five or six people each. Allow time for each member to share briefly. Then solicit some responses from the groups. If some of the following are not offered, you may wish to add them:
— The Scriptures enrich our faith life because we come to know God in and through Jesus Christ and the Holy Spirit.
— Scripture is a source of our prayer and reflection.
— We may pray scriptural prayers, such as the psalms or the Our Father.
— The Scriptures are part of the celebration of the Eucharist. In the liturgy of the word when the Scriptures are read, "Christ is present in his word because it is he who speaks when sacred Scripture is read in the church" (*Constitution on the Sacred Liturgy,* No. 7).
— Hearing the word challenges us to live the word.

2. Read the Parable of the Sower (Mark 4:1-9) silently and then listen as your leader or another member of the group reads it aloud.

2. Explain to the group that the parable describes the typical way that seed was sown in Palestine. Sowing took place before plowing, so the sower actually intends to scatter seed on the footpath, the rocky ground and even among thorns. As the ground is plowed up, the seed is plowed in. Then direct the groups to continue with the sharing questions in their Workbooks.

3. Give two or three words to describe these images:

footpath

rocky ground

thorns

good soil

4. Which of these images best represents the obstacles you face to hearing the word of God?

5. "Let those who have ears to hear me, hear!" What do you think it means to hear?

CLOSING PRAYER

Time: 10 minutes

Preparation

Place a large candle at the center of the group. If possible, tapers should be passed out to the participants. For the reading of the gospel, two participants should be asked to read the parts labeled "reader" and "Jesus."

A Call to Remember

Leader:

"Christ is present in his word because it is he who speaks when sacred Scripture is read in the church." Our teacher is the risen Christ and the Spirit-Paraclete whom he promised. We are the church. Let us respond by praying this doxology:

> *All:*
> Now to God, who is able to accomplish far more than all we can ask or can even imagine, by the power at work within us, to God be glory in the church and in Christ Jesus for all generations, forever and ever. Amen.

Leader:

More than we can ever imagine! Let us listen to the incredible good news of the resurrection, which is the beginning of the New Testament, the new covenant.

Gospel

If possible, darken the room a bit.

> (All stand, holding tapers and facing the large candle at the center of the group.)
>
> *Reader:*
> The Good News of Jesus Christ, raised and with us here!
>
> (All now light their tapers from the large candle and then listen to an adaptation of Luke 24:13-24.)

Reader:

On that very day, two disciples were journeying toward Emmaus. Jesus drew near and walked with them, but they did not recognize him.

Jesus:

What are you discussing as you walk along?

(Pause for reflection.)

Reader:
Some women from our group reported that they had seen angels who announced that Jesus was alive. Then some of us went to the tomb and found things just as the women had said, but they did not see Jesus.

Jesus:
How foolish you are and slow of heart.

(Pause for reflection.)

Reader:
Then, beginning with Moses and all the prophets, he interpreted for them what referred to him in the Scriptures. They urged him to stay with them, for it was getting near evening. While he was with them at table, he took bread, said the blessing, broke it, and gave it to them. With that their eyes were opened and they recognized him, but he vanished. Then they said to each other: Were not our hearts burning within in us as he spoke to us on the road and opened the Scriptures for us?

(Pause for reflection.)

Concluding Prayer

Leader:
Let us pray: (Pause)
Open our hearts to know you, to recognize you, to learn from you, Lord Jesus. Let our hearts burn within us as we meet you on the journey we begin tonight. We praise you and thank you for your gift of the Spirit who is guiding us to all truth and fullness of life: knowing you and the one who sent you. And so we pray:

All:
Our Mother and Father who art in heaven . . . . For the kingdom, the power and the glory are yours, now and forever. Amen.

Leader:
Let us go in peace to love and serve the Lord.

All:
Thanks be to God.

Song

"Grant to us, O Lord"

FOLLOW-UP

A. Journaling

Read the parable of the sower and the seed, Mark 4:1-9.

What part of your life is the path that is beaten down?

Where is the rocky soil in your life?

What are the thorns that exist?

Do you recognize and can you identify the good soil in yourself?

Which of the obstacles to hearing the word of God do you need to overcome? What can you do to accomplish this?

B. Additional Resources

1. Read: Pheme Perkins, *Reading the New Testament,* Chapter 1, ''Why Study the Bible,'' pp. 1-22.

2. Read: Anthony Marinelli, *Understanding the Gospels,* Chapter 1, ''Formation of the Gospels,'' pp. 3-14.

3. Read: Raymond E. Brown, S.S., *Responses to 101 Questions on the Bible,* Questions 38-44.

4. Read: *The Catholic Study Bible,* ''The Bible in Catholic Life,'' RG 16-30.

C. Further Reading

The New Jerome Biblical Commentary, "Recent Developments in New Testament Scholarship," 70:79-84.

Philip A. Cunningham, *Jesus and the Evangelists,* "The Origins of the Gospels," pp. 9-25.

2. The Life of Jesus

Preparation

- Read Perkins, Chapter 3, "The Life of Jesus."
- Try to read as many of the references mentioned in the text as you can find time for. The following will be the focus of learning activities in this session:

> *Miracle stories* (cf. pp. 52-54 of the text)
> Mark 1:23-28 (exorcisms)
> Matthew 8:28-34
> Mark 6:30-44 (feeding the crowds)
> Mark 8:1-10
> Matthew 8:5-13 (healing)
>
> *Pronouncements* (cf. pp. 55-57 of the text)
> Mark 7:24-30
> Matthew 5:21-28
>
> *Teaching* (cf. pp. 67-68 of the text)
> Mark 2:23-28
> Mark 7:15
> Luke 6:27-36
> Luke 4:18-21

- Reflect on the FOCUS statement and REVIEW OF CONTENTS Questions.

General Goals:
— To help participants realize that the gospels are not historical documents as we would understand history today.
— To enable participants to recognize that the gospels are records of the life of Jesus as it was remembered and preached by those who had come to believe in him. The gospels witness to the initiation of the new age of salvation by Jesus; people's lives were changed and continue to be changed today.

FOCUS

Most of what we know about Jesus comes to us from the gospels. The gospels, however, do not give us an historical account of Jesus' life, as we understand history today. They are not modern-style biographies. On the other hand, the gospels do contain remembrances of Jesus' words and actions.

In seeking Jesus through the gospels, it is very helpful to understand how the gospels came to be. Much of what is contained in the gospels as we have them was originally handed on from community to community of believers *orally*. Stories were told of Jesus' miracles. His sayings were collected as his followers remembered them. The circumstances of his death were also recalled. All of these remembrances about Jesus were interpreted in the light of who the first Christians experienced Jesus to be: a turning point in their lives, the One who brought salvation, the Son of God. So, the life of Jesus that we read in the gospels is told through the eyes of faith. What was finally written down was what the first communities of Christians remembered and came to understand about the meaning (not just the facts) of Jesus' life, death, and resurrection.

OPENING PRAYER

Time: 5 minutes

Preparation
Refer the participants to their workbooks where they will find the text of Psalm 81. Let them know which side will be right and which will be left.

Leader:
Please open your hands, palms up, on your lap. Let your hands be filled with the burdens of today: the worries, disappointments, frustrations, as I pray from Psalm 81:
    I hear an unfamiliar voice saying:
    "I took the heavy loads off your backs;

I let you put down your work-baskets.
When you were in trouble and called to me
and I saved you;
I set you free, in the open.
From my hiding place in the storm I answer you."

(Pause for reflection)

Leader:
Let the Lord take these burdens from you.

(Pause for reflection)

Leader:
Let us respond together by praying the rest of Psalm 81.

Psalm 81

Left Side:
Shout with joy to God our defender!
Sing praise to the God of Israel!
Start the music, play the tambourine,
play pleasant music on harps and lyres,
blow the horn for the festival.

Right Side:
This is the law in Israel,
the command from our God.
God commanded this when God marched out on our
        behalf,
setting us free from slavery.

Leader:
Listen, my people, to me!
Oh my people, how I wish you would listen to me!
You must never worship another God.
It is I who led you from slavery.
Open your mouth and I will feed you.
I would feed you with the finest wheat
and satisfy you with honey.

All:
We open our ears and mouths and hearts and minds
tonight, our God, as best we can. Thank you for freeing
us from so many burdens that we might listen to the
good news more eagerly, more openly, with music in our
hearts. We pray this through Christ our Lord. Amen.

REVIEW OF CONTENTS

Objectives: That participants demonstrate their knowledge, through discussion, of 1) evidence of the oral transmission of the gospels, i.e., inherited forms of exorcism and pronouncement stories, and 2) evidence of the faith context in which the stories about Jesus were preserved and handed on.

Time: 25 minutes

1. The early disciples of Jesus did not use writing to remember stories about him. In order to aid their memory they fitted many of the stories into forms or patterns that were already common in their culture.

a. What are the three components of the pattern of an exorcism story? (Check Perkins, p. 53)

1. Demonstration of the symptoms of the illness
2. Verbal conflict between the demon and the exorcist
3. Departure of the demon with some kind of violence

b. Examine Matthew 8:28-34. Identify the three components.

1. vs. 28
2. vs. 29-31
3. vs. 32

Despite the fact that this story of the exorcism of demons by Jesus is similar in pattern to other exorcism stories, (see that told by Perkins, pp. 52-53), are there any significant differences?

Here the difference is mainly that Jesus is not soliciting a monetary reward. Notice also, however, that the demons address Jesus as "Son of God." As Perkins points out, this is evidence that the story was told among Christians to convince non-believers of Jesus' identity.

2. Read Mark 6:30-44 and Mark 8:1-10.

a. What are the similarities between these two accounts of Jesus' feeding a large number of people?

There was a large crowd. Jesus felt pity for them. A small amount of food was available. The disciples did not seem to expect what Jesus would do. Jesus blessed and broke the loaves. There were leftovers. After the event, Jesus got into a boat with his disciples.

b. What evidence do scholars have for suggesting that these are two different versions of the same event? (Note chapter 8, verse 4. Do the disciples seem to have experienced a similar happening before?)

The disciples were just as bewildered and surprised in the second account of the multiplication of the loaves as they were the first time. They don't seem to have had this experience before.

c. If these are not two different events, how does one explain the differences between the accounts? (See Perkins, p. 54)

A collection of miracle stories seems to have existed and was used by Mark in the composition of his gospel. Often different versions of the same miracle existed, as seems to be the case here. Perkins refers to other examples as well. These versions resulted from inaccurate memory and/or adaptation for pastoral reasons.

3. Comparing accounts of events in Jesus' life as they are told by different evangelists often gives us clues to the "faith context," that is, the particular problems or needs of individual Christian communities. Preachers or missionaries adapted details of the story to suit these needs without changing the essential message or spirit of Jesus' life.

Review Mark 7:24-30 and Matthew 15:21-28, as compared by Perkins on pp. 56-57.

a. Identify the pattern of a pronouncement story (p. 55).

Tension or problem (Mk 7:24-28, Mt 15:21-27)
Wisdom of the hero demonstrated (Mk 7:29-30, Mt 15:28)

b. Note the differences in detail. What do these differences tell us about the community in which Matthew's version was preserved? (p. 57)

Such details in Matthew's version as the expansion of the obstacles that Jesus presents to the woman and Jesus' explicit praising of her faith—which itself seems to have healed her daughter—indicate a certain context for the story. A pagan woman is capable of faith that wins salvation from Jesus. Not only Jews belong to Jesus' kingdom. The many obstacles may indicate the problems that the Christian communities had to deal with in order to come to this conclusion.

4. Jesus' followers experienced in their association with him that a new age of salvation was breaking into the world. Jesus' teachings often reflect the radical nature of this new age.

What does each of the following teachings of Jesus suggest about the kind of new age the first Christians experienced in Jesus? (See Perkins, pp. 67-68)
    Mark 2:23-28
    Mark 7:15
    Luke 6:27-36
    Luke 4:18-21

Responses should include such comments as: Jesus placed human need, healing, and salvation before observance of the law. Jesus disassociated himself from the Pharisees for whom holiness was the adherence to the strictest interpretation of the law. Jesus challenges us to the highest ideals (love of enemies, for example); his law does not describe what most people do. Jesus is initiating a new age in which the old order is destroyed and a new one established—the sick are healed, the blind see, and the poor are raised up.

VIDEO

Objective: That participants appreciate something of the milieu of first-century Christians in which stories about Jesus were first told and preached.

Time: 20 minutes

The World of Jesus and the Gospels.

As you view the video, make note of the following:

Who were:

Pharisees _____

Sadducees _____

Essenes _____

Zealots _____

Samaritans _____

Video Outline

The World of Jesus and the Gospels

1. Palestine under Roman Rule
   a. Herod
   b. Jewish expectation of the Messiah

2. The Jesus of History
   a. His Jewishness
   b. His knowledge of the Scriptures

3. Judaism at the Time of Jesus
   a. Pharisees: Mostly laymen, believed in the strict interpretation and observance of the law
   b. Scribes: Educated laymen who were experts in the Jewish law
   c. Essenes: A sect of Jews who lived mostly in the desert and rejected the Temple worship of Jerusalem
   d. Sadducees: The aristocratic party from which the Chief Priests and Sanhedrin were selected
   e. Zealots: A Jewish sect seeking independence from Rome through revolution
   f. Samaritans: People who lived in the region of Samaria, despised by the Jews and considered heretical
   g. Sabbath Observance and the Synagogue
   h. The Temple

BREAK

(10 minutes)

LEARNING ACTIVITY

Objective: That participants recognize the impact that the experience of Jesus had on the lives of those who first came to believe in him.

Time: 25 minutes

This exercise should be done in groups of four or five. Working in groups not only instills more confidence in dealing with the texts, but also allows individuals to benefit from others' insights into the readings. It would be good to stress the importance of this as you assign the exercise. At the end of the exercise, have representatives of each group read their profiles.

The Gospels are witnesses to the faith experience of the first Christians. Jesus brought them new life. The demons of the old life were being cast out. The power of God was manifested in a new way.

Choose one of the following "first Christians." (Your leader may assign one to your group.) Then read the appropriate New Testament passages.

Peter
Luke 5:1-11
Matthew 10:1-5
Matthew 14:22-33
Matthew 16:13-16
Luke 22:54-62
Acts 2 (esp. 40-41)

Mary, Jesus' Mother
Luke 1:34-38
Luke 1:46-55
John 19:25-27
Acts 1:12-14

Nicodemus
John 3:1-21
John 7:50-51

The Samaritan Woman
John 4:4-42

Mary Magdalene
Luke 8:1-3
Luke 7:36-50 (which may refer to Mary Magdalene)
Matthew 27:56, 61
Mark 16:1
John 20:1-18

1. Make a note of and discuss

a. the nature of the person's first recorded encounter with Jesus

b. how that person's life was touched and changed by Jesus

c. any indication of the further effect that person's experience of Jesus had on others

2. Relying on your reading and review of Perkins, the video presentation, the specific New Testament references you have just read, and your imagination, construct a profile of your New Testament character. Have one of your group deliver it as a testimony. For example, you would begin, "I am Peter (or Mary, etc.) . . ." and proceed to tell his or her story.

This exercise should help to give a sense of reality to the New Testament characters. Real people with real lives were affected by Jesus. For some, the change may have been spectacular; for others (most), it was gradual and quiet. Peter's humanness is evident not only in his continual need for assurance (Mt 15:28-31) and his lack of courage (Lk 22:54-56) on the one hand, but also in his enthusiasm (Mt 16:13-20) and readiness to keep trying on the other. Despite his weakness, he becomes an important leader in the establishment of Christianity.

Nicodemus seems puzzled by or perhaps attracted to Jesus. There is no open declaration of his faith in the gospels, but it seems that conversion was happening. He speaks for justice to Jesus even at his own risk (Jn 7:50-51). His initial encounter with Jesus, as reported by John, involved seeking intellectual conviction. His showing up to anoint Jesus' body may be an indication of a quiet inner search to understand what Jesus was all about.

Both the story of Mary Magdalene and the story of Mary, the mother of Jesus, are well known and have been widely popularized. Encourage the participants to listen carefully to what the texts actually say, however.

The story of the Samaritan woman may serve to illustrate the presence of Jesus in unexpected and ordinary parts of our lives (the regular chore of going to the well). The surprising element for the woman is that she (a Samaritan and a woman) would be receiving attention from this man. He puts her in touch with her own life and invites her to be part of a new life. She in turn invites others to come and see the source of this new life.

You may need to offer some further helpful questions to enable groups to feel comfortable with the latter part of the exercise. For example, begin by recalling some of the "world of Jesus." How might these characters have lived from day to day? What might have been their occupations, their concerns? What was new about Jesus? Add appropriate details to reconstruct the first time they encountered Jesus. How did their lives change as a result of that encounter? How were their previous relationships changed? Did they have new hopes? A new vision?

FAITH SHARING

Objective: That participants work toward recognizing that they too, like the first Christians, are called to an experience of Jesus that can (and may already) have a powerful impact on their own lives and on those with whom they share their lives.

Time: 25 minutes

Continuing in the same small groups, invite participants to share their reflections on these questions.

1. Reflect for a moment on the testimonies of New Testament Christians that you have just heard. Which of these first Christians (if any) appeals to you most? Why?

2. As was the case with the New Testament Christians you read about, Jesus' power works differently for different people. For Peter, it was gradual, with some major setbacks. For the Samaritan woman, it was more dramatic and immediate. How do you experience Jesus' presence in your life?

CLOSING PRAYER

Time: 10 minutes

Preparation
A clear bowl filled with water should be placed in the center of the group. Instruct the participants that at the conclusion of this prayer service each one will approach the water and dip into it to make the sign of the cross. Some appropriate background music would enhance this moment.

A Call to Remember

Leader:
"A new age of salvation is breaking into the world." Salvation here comes from the Hebrew word *yesh,* meaning to be given space, room to grow. Sometimes we translate the Hebrew word *shalom*—meaning peace, wholeness, health, and integrity—as salvation.

Reader:
A reading from the words of the prophets.
   "My plans for you are plans of *shalom,* says the Lord." (Jer 29:11)
   "With joy you will draw water at the fountain of salvation." (Is 12:3)

Leader:
The name of Jesus, *yeshua,* is the Hebrew word for salvation. As Matthew tells us, "He will save his people from their sins" (Mt 1:21). Let us respond to this good news.

Response:
Lord Jesus, thank you for yourself, for your Spirit, a fountain of living water springing up from deep within us. Please keep opening us to the depths of yourself, our self, the depths of your salvation, and our discipleship. We pray in the company of your first disciples:

Litany

Leader:	*All:*
Peter,	Pray with us.
Mary Magdalene,	Pray with us.
Nicodemus,	Pray with us.
Mary of Nazareth,	Pray with us.
Syrophoenician woman,	Pray with us.

(Add your own favorite New Testament disciples)

Leader:
Lord Jesus,

All:
Pray with us.

All:
Our Father and Mother, who art in heaven . . . . For the kingdom and the power and the glory are yours, now and forever. Amen.

Prayer

Leader:
In closing tonight, let us draw water at the fountain of salvation, and mark ourselves with the sign of the cross, the sign of our discipleship.

(Each one approaches the water and, touching it, makes the sign of the cross.)

Leader:
Let us go in peace to love and serve the Lord.

All:
Thanks be to God!

FOLLOW-UP

A. Journaling

Think again of Jesus clashing with the demons and over-coming them. Mary Magdalene is described as a disciple from whom seven demons had been cast out. Write a prayer or reflection in which you acknowledge the modern demons that affect your life. Imagine your life without the influence of these demons. Are there steps you can take to live in such a new age of salvation initiated by Jesus?

B. Additional Resources

1. Read: Pheme Perkins, *Reading the New Testament,* Chapter 1, "The World of Jesus," pp. 23-50.

2. Read Anthony Marinelli, *Understanding the Gospels,* Chapter 2, "The New Testament World," pp. 15-31.

3. Read *The Catholic Study Bible,* "Introduction to the Synoptic Gospels," RG 386-388.

4. Using the Hammond *Atlas of the Bible Lands,* examine the maps on pages 24-25. Locate Palestine and Jerusalem on the map of the Roman world. What is Palestine called? What is its status with regard to Rome? Approximately how far is it from Jerusalem to Rome?

C. Further Reading

The New Jerome Biblical Commentary, "Jesus: Origins and Ministry," 78:11-24; "Pharisees, Sadducees, Essenes," 75:146-151.

Philip A. Cunningham, *Jesus and the Evangelists,* "A Profile of the Ministry of Jesus," pp. 125-139.

3. The Preaching of Jesus

Preparation

- Read Perkins, Chapter 4, "The Preaching of Jesus."
- Read as many of the following references in Chapter 4 of the companion text as you can find time for:

Matthew 5:33-37	Mark 4:26-32
5:43-48	10:13-16
6:9-15	12:28-34
6:19-21	
7:1-5	Luke 7:36-50
9:3-13	15:1-32
11:16-19	17:11-21
13:44-46	
18:21-35	
20:1-15	

- Reflect on the FOCUS statement and the REVIEW OF CONTENTS questions.

General Goals:
— To enable participants to understand that the reign of God is the key-note of the preaching of Jesus.
— To appreciate the preaching of Jesus as a call to discipleship and a call to transformation of one's life and world.
— To explore the ways in which Jesus preached the reign of God in the context of his life and ministry in order to understand the message for our lives today.

OPENING PRAYER

Time: 5 minutes

Preparation
The prayer leader need not be the leader of the session. Hopefully, leadership in prayer will circulate among the group members who are comfortable with it, just as the readers will also change.

Leader:
Jesus preached and so made present in his world the saving presence of God. The reign of God is this saving presence and action of God on our behalf. Let us respond to this good news by praying Psalm 85 (verses 8-14):

Right side:
Show us, O Lord, your kindness,
And grant us your salvation.

Left side:
I will hear what God proclaims.
Our God proclaims peace:

Peace to God's people, the faithful ones!
Peace to those who put their hope in God!

Right side:
Near indeed is God's salvation to us who love God,
Glory, dwelling in our midst.

Left side:
Kindness and truth shall meet, justice and peace shall kiss.
Truth shall spring out of the earth
and justice look down from heaven.

Right side:
The Lord will give us blessings.
Justice shall walk before our God
and salvation along the way of God's steps.

Leader:
This word of God does what it says: kindness, truth,
justice, peace meet in our hearts, and in our group. Let us
pause, and pray that such good news might sink in and
bear fruit . . . . We ask this in Jesus' name.

All:
Amen.

Song

Perhaps just the chorus of the St. Louis Jesuits'
"Lift Up Your Hearts to the Lord."

REVIEW OF CONTENTS

Objective: To enable the participants to review and to reflect on the characteristics of the reign of God in the preaching of Jesus.

Time: 25 minutes

Divide the participants into small groups and assign each group one of the Scripture passages in their Workbooks. Ask them to decide what the passage says about the reign of God. After allowing sufficient time to discuss the passage, ask for a representative from each group to report. As the groups report you may want to emphasize:

— the basic message preached by Jesus was the coming of the reign of God;

— there is no clear-cut definition of the reign of God; the reign of God refers to God's saving presence in the world;

— some of the characteristics of the reign of God are forgiveness, reconciliation, justice and peace;

— Jesus preached that the reign of God existed wherever there were persons whose lives had been transformed by his teaching and efforts were being made to transform oppressive and dehumanizing social structures;

— the reign of God is not only in this world but will be completed in the future coming of the kingdom;

— the reign of God is also called the kingdom of God.

What characteristic of the reign of God is most evident in each of these sayings and stories?

1. Luke 17:11-21

2. Mark 10:13-16

3. Luke 15:8-10

4. Matthew 6:19-21

5. Mark 4:26-29

30

1. *Luke 17:11-21:* One of the ways in which Jesus proclaimed the reign of God was through his sayings. Here he says that if the Pharisees had been open to God's presence, they would have recognized God in the words and deeds of Jesus, particularly in the cure of the lepers (Luke 17:11-19). God's reign is in the here and now, if we have the eyes to see.

2. *Mark 10:13-16:* Pronouncement stories were another means that Jesus used to announce the coming of the reign of God. This pronouncement story teaches that the kingdom must be recognized and received as a gift, the way a child receives a gift, that is, with simplicity and openness.

3. *Luke 15:8-10:* Parables were yet another means that Jesus employed to preach the reign of God. Here Jesus says God is like a woman who has lost a coin and is so overjoyed when what has been lost is found that she calls others to celebrate. God's love and mercy are given to all people; no one is outside of God's mercy.

4. *Matthew 6:19-21:* Here Jesus uses a wisdom saying. It brings together the ordinary concerns of everyday life with commitment to the reign of God. This saying reminds us that "you can't take it with you," but that the energy put into deeds of kindness and concern for others, as well as acts of peacemaking and forgiveness, manifest the reign of God both now and in the future.

5. *Mark 4:26-29:* Although the focus of the parable is on the coming reign of God, the fact that the kingdom of God is also a present reality is described by the seed and its growth. The emphasis here is on God's action.

VIDEO

Objectives: To help participants grow in their understanding of Jesus' parables about the reign of God, the image of God found in Jesus' parables, and the cost of becoming one of Jesus' disciples.

Time: 20 minutes

The Reign of God and the Parables of Jesus

As you view this video, make note of the following:

What characteristics of the reign of God are revealed in these parables?

a. The Yeast _____

_____

b. The Great Feast _____

_____

c. The Laborers in the Field _____

_____

2. What are the qualities of a disciple described in these parables?

a. The Rich Man and Lazarus _____

_____

b. The Good Samaritan _____

_____

Video Outline

The Reign of God and the Parables of Jesus

1. Jesus' preaching about the reign of God
    a. Old Testament background for the reign of God
    b. Jesus' parables best express the reign of God
    c. The Yeast: God's power hidden in the world
    d. The Great Feast: the reign of God is like a banquet
    e. The Laborers in the Field: the reign of God is a gift

2. Jesus' understanding of God
    a. Abba
    b. The Prodigal Son: God is forgiving

3. The cost of entering into God's reign
    a. "Repent and believe the good news!"
    b. The Treasure in the Field: a new way of living
    c. The two greatest commandments
    d. The Rich Man and Lazarus: love of your neighbor
    e. The Good Samaritan: love of your enemies

BREAK

(10 minutes)

LEARNING ACTIVITY

Objective: To reflect on the meaning of discipleship in the Lord's Prayer.

Time: 25 minutes

Ask the group to work in pairs and to determine a characteristic of discipleship found in each petition of the prayer. At the completion of the task, ask the participants to share their findings in the large group.

What quality of discipleship is found in each petition of the Lord's Prayer?

The Lord's Prayer	Characteristics of a Disciple
(Mt 6:9-13)	
Our Father, who art in heaven, hallowed be thy name;	
Thy kingdom come; thy will be done on earth as it is in heaven.	
Give us this day our daily bread;	
and forgive us our debts as we also have forgiven our debtors;	
And lead us not into temptation, but deliver us from evil.	

Here are some of the many possible qualities of a disciple that could be mentioned along with each petition:

Our Father, who art in heaven, hallowed be thy name: The disciple prays *our* Father, recognizing him or herself to be in a community of believers. The disciple shares in Jesus' own relationship to the Father. The disciple is a son or daughter of God. The disciple experiences God as a loving personal presence, and God's love like the love of a father or mother. The disciple recognizes God as transcendent, beyond the limits of human experience, "in heaven." The disciple prays, praising God's name.

Thy kingdom come; thy will be done on earth as it is in heaven: The disciple awaits the coming of the kingdom, recognizing that only God can bring all human longings and sufferings to a conclusion. The disciple prays for God's will to be done on earth, both in the disciple's own life and that of all people. This is not a passive prayer, "May your will be done to me," but an active one, "May I do your will."

Give us this day our daily bread: The disciple depends on God for all things, both physical and spiritual. The disciple lives in the present, trusting in God for today and not worrying about tomorrow.

And forgive us our debts as we also have forgiven our debtors: The disciple is a sinner, relying on God's forgiveness. The disciple must therefore forgive others.

And lead us not into temptation, but deliver us from evil: The disciple prays to be preserved from temptation and sin. The disciple recognizes that even the ability to remain faithful is a gift of God.

FAITH SHARING

Objective: To reflect on forgiveness and reconciliation as marks of the kingdom and qualities of a disciple.

Time: 25 minutes

Using the text in the Workbook, read the Parable of the Unmerciful Servant (Mt 18:21-35). Ask for volunteers to read the following parts: Peter, Jesus, the king, the unmerciful servant and the fellow servant.

The Parable of the Unmerciful Servant

Narrator: Then Peter came up and asked him,

Peter: "Lord, when my brother wrongs me, how often, must I forgive him? Seven times?"

Jesus: "No, not seven times; I say, seventy times seven times."

Narrator: That is why the reign of God may be said to be like a king who decided to settle accounts with his officials. When he began his auditing, one was brought in who owed him a huge amount. As he had no way of paying it, his master ordered him to be sold, along with his wife, his children, and all his property in payment of the debt. At that, the official prostrated himself in homage and said,

Official: "My lord, be patient with me and I will pay you back in full."

Narrator: Moved with pity the master let the official go and wrote off the debt. But when that same official went out he met a fellow servant who owed him a mere fraction of what he himself owed. He seized him and throttled him.

Official: "Pay back what you owe."

Narrator: His fellow servant dropped to his knees and began to plead with him,

Servant: "Just give me time, and I will pay you back in full!"

Narrator: But he would hear none of it. Instead he had him put in jail until he paid back what he owed. When his fellow servants saw what had happened they were badly shaken, and went to their master to report the whole incident. His master sent for him and said:

King: "I cancelled your entire debt when you pleaded with me. Should you not have dealt mercifully with your fellow servant, as I dealt with you?"

Narrator: Then in anger the master handed him over to the torturers until he paid back all that he owed.

Jesus: "My heavenly Father will treat you in exactly the same way unless each of you forgives your brother (or sister) from your heart."

Now, in small groups or in pairs, have the participants share their own personal responses to the Reflection Questions.

Reflection Questions

1. What connection do you see between this parable and the Lord's Prayer?

2. Why do you think the unmerciful servant failed to grant his fellow servant's request?

3. Why would Jesus tell a story of forgiveness in which the person forgiven was not changed by the experience?

4. Is there any relationship in your life that this parable addresses?

CLOSING PRAYER

Time: 10 minutes

Preparation
The leader will need to procure seeds, the symbol for this session. They may be flower seeds or vegetable seeds, perhaps potato eyes from the leader's dinner preparations that night, or apple seeds from lunch.

A Call to Remember

Leader:
The reign of God "is God's saving presence revealed in Jesus' healings and exorcisms and in Jesus' sayings and parables . . . an experience of redemption and reconciliation." God's saving presence is made visible and tangible in Jesus' own self.

Reader:
A reading from the gospel according to Mark (4:26-29).

All:
Glory to you, O Lord.

Leader:
Let us respond by remembering a powerful word which Jesus once spoke and still speaks to us tonight, a word which we want to take root in us. When you have remembered, speak the word or the sentence out loud. I will then give you a seed to plant at home, a symbol of God's reign taking root in your own life.
(Allow a few moments of silence.)

A Call to Grow

Have each participant speak his or her word or sentence. Then, after each one speaks . . .

The leader gives each participant a seed, saying: May the word of Christ grow in your mind and heart. Each responds: Amen!

Leader:
Let us pray together, in the words of Matthew, the Our
Father . . .

Direct the group to the text in the Learning Activity step. (Do not use
"Mother" or the concluding doxology: "For the kingdom, the power . . .")

Leader:
Let us go in peace to love and serve the Lord and be
signs of God's reign in our world.

All:
Thanks be to God!

Concluding Song

The song can be the same as that used for the opening prayer, or something like: "Let Peace Reign in Our Hearts")

REMINDER FOR NEXT WEEK:
We will use your own versions of the Lord's Prayer to be
written in the follow-up journal exercise in our opening
prayer next week.

FOLLOW-UP

A. Journaling

Rewrite the Lord's Prayer in your own words.

Or, reread the parable of the unmerciful servant in terms of your own life.

- Have you been forgiven and yet refused to give forgiveness?

- Have you ever made unrealistic demands on another? What are reasons why you have withheld forgiveness?

- What does the parable say to your life?

- Or perhaps you have tried to reconcile and your attempt has been rejected? Does the parable say anything to that situation?

Or, what contemporary situations calling for forgiveness and reconciliation come to mind in reading one of the parables? Write a parable for today. How does the message of the parable apply to this current situation? Is there a way in which your study group could help this situation?

B. Additional Resources

1. Read: Anthony Marinelli, *Understanding the Gospels,* Chapter 3, ''The Coming of the Reign of God,'' pp. 33-53.

2. Read: Raymond E. Brown, S.S., *Responses to 101 Questions on the Bible,* Questions 45-51.

C. Further Reading

The New Jerome Biblical Commentary, "The Parables of Jesus," 81:59-88; "The Miracles of Jesus," 81:91-117.

Philip A. Cunningham, *Jesus and the Evangelists,* "Parables of God's Reign," pp. 140-158; "God's Reign and the Mission of Jesus," pp. 159-174.

4. The Resurrection of Jesus

Preparation

- Read Perkins, Chapter 5, "The Resurrection of Jesus."
- Read the accounts of the resurrection appearances in Mark 16:1-20; Matthew 28:1-20; Luke 24; John 20.
- Reflect on the FOCUS statement and the REVIEW OF CONTENTS questions.

General Goals:
— To help participants read and reflect upon the resurrection narratives in order to see how the disciples came to faith in the risen Christ and how belief in the resurrection transformed their lives.
— To gain insight into the meaning of the Resurrection for us today.

FOCUS

In the accounts of the empty tomb and the post-resurrection appearance narratives, there are two key aspects: the empty tomb and the disciples' experience of the risen Christ. The discovery of the empty tomb left the disciples "half joyful, half fearful," and unable to comprehend what had happened. The Easter appearances of Jesus are the primary way in which the disciples came to know that Jesus was raised. Mary Magdalene, Mary, the mother of James, the other Mary, Peter and all the other disciples have seen for themselves and have come to believe. Through their testimony, we believe. The disciples interpreted the events that they experienced in the light of the Scriptures. This experience of the resurrection, in turn, gave new meaning to the Scriptures.

This session will focus on the background to the resurrection and explore those aspects which made it difficult for the disciples to grasp the reality of resurrection. We will look at the narratives of the empty tomb to discern their importance in building up resurrection faith and see what it is the gospels tell us about the risen Christ in the appearance stories.

OPENING PRAYER

Time: 5 minutes

Preparation
The leader will need to check how many participants brought their own version of the Lord's Prayer with them. If many people forgot, the group might stay as a large whole; if many came prepared, it might be better to divide into small groups so that each group has about three different personal versions. After the group is assembled and some quieting background music is gradually lowered, the leader begins:

Gathering Prayer

Leader:
Let us pray . . .

(Pause)

Lord Jesus, come and pray with us. Risen Lord, be as present to us as you were to your disciples on the road to Emmaus. Please bring us the peace you offered them on Easter evening as we gather to pray with you. We, who so often use the words you taught us to pray, ask you now to pray in us and use our words as we pray your prayer, the Lord's Prayer. We ask you this in the power of your Spirit.

All:
Amen!

Leader:
Those who are prepared, please pray your own version of the Lord's Prayer now, leaving some moments of reflection after each one prays.

Song

The concluding song can be begun softly as one of the small groups finishes, and as other groups finish, they can join the song. Use "Praise God" to the tune of "Amazing Grace," or "Peace Is Flowing Like a River," or any other song which will not require hymn books.

REVIEW OF CONTENTS

Objective: To compare and contrast the narratives of the empty tomb in order to see how the variants in Matthew 28 and Luke 24 answer the objections that outsiders may have made against Christian preaching of the resurrection.

Time: 25 minutes

1. Read one of the accounts of the empty tomb narratives: Mark 16:1-8; Matthew 28:1-20; Luke 24; Mark 16:9-20; John 20. Use these questions to guide your reading:

When did the story take place?

Who were the women involved?

Why did the women come to the tomb?

What was seen?

What was said?

How did the women react?

1. The participants have been asked to read the resurrection accounts as preparation for the session. Assign each person in the group one of the accounts of the empty tomb: Mark 16:1-8; Matthew 28:1-20; Luke 24; Mark 16:9-20; and John 20. Give the group two or three minutes to look over the text in the Bible. Then ask them to answer each of the questions in their workbooks using words from the gospel text.

The following chart compares the gospel versions.

THE NARRATIVES OF THE EMPTY TOMB

	MARK 16:1-8	MATTHEW 28:1-20	LUKE 24	MARK 16:9-20	JOHN 20
WHEN?	very early; first day of the week	growing light; first day of the week	early dawn; first day of the week	early; first day of the week	still dark; early; first day of the week
WHO?	Mary Magdalene; Mary, the mother of James; Salome	Mary Magdalene; other Mary	Mary Magdalene	Mary Magdalene	Mary Magdalene; another? ("we" in verse 2)
WHY?	brought spices; came to anoint	came to see tomb	spices from Friday; took spices along		
WHAT SEEN?	stone rolled back; youth sitting on right	earthquake; angel descended; he rolled back stone; sat on it outside	stone rolled back; two men standing inside	Jesus	stone rolled away; later two angels sitting inside
WHAT SAID?	youth said not to fear; Jesus is risen; tell the disciples he is going to Galilee	angel said not to fear; Jesus is risen; tell the disciples he is going to Galilee	men asked questions; recalled prophecy made in Scriptures		later angels asked: Why do you weep?
HOW?	fled trembling; told no one	went away quickly, with fear	returned; told the eleven and the rest		went and told Peter; "other" disciple; went and told follower

2. What are the assertions that are made in the gospel passages?

— The tomb was empty.
— An angel (youth, men, two angels) gave the women the message that Jesus was risen.
— Even when the disciples were told that Jesus was raised, they could not understand what had happened.

3. Do the gospel accounts make the empty tomb a proof of the resurrection? Why or why not?

The empty tomb was not put forward as proof of the resurrection nor can it prove resurrection. The accounts make two simple assertions: the tomb is empty; Jesus is raised from the dead.

In Mark, there is no attempt to use the empty tomb as proof, or Mark would not have used women as witnesses. The testimony of women was unacceptable in the culture of the time.

In Matthew, there is conjecture that the tomb was empty because the disciples came during the night and stole the body away (Mt 28:13). This would seem to indicate that the Jews were forced to admit that the body was not in the tomb and therefore needed to find some other explanation other than resurrection for the phenomenon.

VIDEO

Objective: To enable participants to gain an understanding of how Jesus' disciples may have interpreted his death and resurrection by drawing upon and expanding the resources of their Jewish tradition.

Time: 20 minutes

Interpreting the Resurrection

As you view this video, make note of the following:

1. What was meant by the suffering of the righteous?

_____

2. What did the Pharisees believe about the resurrection on the last day?

_____

What did the Sadducees believe?

_____

With which group did Jesus agree on this question?

_____

3. How did the appearance of the risen Jesus affect his disciples?

_____

_____

Video Outline

Interpreting the Resurrection

1. How did the disciples understand the death of Jesus?
   a. the death of Jesus as a time of despair
   b. death as a curse (Dt 21:23)
   c. the suffering of the righteous (2 Mac 7:1-9; Wis 3:1-3; Dan 12:1-3)
   d. the resurrection on the last day: Pharisees vs. Sadducees

2. How did the disciples understand the resurrection of Jesus?
   a. faith based on the experience of seeing him
   b. no basis in Jewish tradition
   c. different from Jesus' raising of the dead
   d. the reality of Jesus
   e. the effect of the presence of the risen Jesus: forgiveness and faith

3. Preaching the risen Jesus
   a. baptism for the forgiveness of sins
   b. the Jews first, then the Gentiles
   c. tension with Judaism (Acts 5:27-39)
   d. faith rests on the resurrection

BREAK

(10 minutes)

LEARNING ACTIVITY

Objective: To reflect on the meaning of the post-resurrection appearance stories for the post-apostolic communities and for us.

Time: 25 minutes

1. Ask the participants to re-convene in the same small groups they formed for the Review of Contents exercise at the beginning of the session and to turn again to that gospel passage. Ask each person to write a response to each of the questions in his or her workbook. Allow about five minutes for this. Then ask them to share with their small group what they have written.

> Reflect again on the passage you read in the Review of Contents section (Mark 16:1-8; Matthew 28:1-20; Mark 16:9-20; Luke 24; John 20).

> What do you consider the fundamental message of the passage to be?

> What images or ideas do you think of when you hear the word resurrection?

> What images does this gospel passage use to convey the idea of resurrection?

> Share what you have written with members of your small group.

2. After a sufficient period of time, elicit responses from the groups about the fundamental message of the gospel passages. These are some of the possible responses that might be made:

Mark: The image of the empty tomb and the message of the "young man" convey that Jesus has conquered death (16:5). There is a reconciliation with the disciples: "Go now and tell the disciples." The disciples will "see"

Jesus in Galilee (16:7). The risen Jesus was revealed to the disciples but was "completely changed in appearance" (16:12).

Luke: Jesus has predicted his death and resurrection (24:6-8); the messiah had to suffer and die in order to fulfill the Scriptures (24:6-8). The disciples recognize Jesus only in the breaking of the bread (24:28-35). Disciples are to be witnesses to the resurrection and to preach the good news to all people (24:46-49).

Matthew: The "mighty earthquake," and the angel of the Lord who resembled a flash of lightning are images that convey that Jesus was raised from the dead. The disciples encountered Jesus as they hurried to tell others. Jesus told them he would meet them in Galilee (28:8-10). The elders and chief priests attempt to discredit the resurrection (28:11-15).

John: Jesus is risen. The cloths which have wrapped the body are all that is found in the tomb (20:5-7). Mary does not immediately recognize Jesus (20:14). Jesus shows the disciples the nail marks in his hands and feet so that they will know that it is he (20:20). All the signs that Jesus worked were so that the disciples might have faith and by faith have life in his name (20:31).

3. Summarize for the group two or three of the conclusions that have emerged from the discussion. For example:

When the disciples found the empty tomb, they could hardly believe that Jesus had been raised; rather, they were confused and frightened. It was only through the revelations of the angel and of Jesus himself that they could believe.

The disciples recognized Jesus but he had been transformed in some way. He was the same but different.

It was through the Scriptures that the disciples gained insight into the meaning of the event of the resurrection. The resurrection, in turn, provided a way of interpreting the Scriptures.

None of stories say that the disciples actually saw Jesus being raised. They simply say that the disciples saw the risen Jesus.

The resurrection can be perceived only in faith.

FAITH SHARING

Objective: To help participants reflect on the ways in which they both encounter the risen Lord and fail to recognize him.

Time: 25 minutes

Read Luke 24:13-35, the appearance of Jesus on the Road to Emmaus. Think of one word that summarizes each one of these sections:

Luke 24:13-16

Luke 24:16-24

Luke 24:25-27

Luke 24:28-32

Luke 24:33-35

Share the word you chose with members of your group. Why did you choose that particular word?

This exercise may also be done to help the participants hear this passage anew. The passage might be read aloud with pauses at each appointed verse during which the participants can write a word.

As time allows, share your response to these questions in your small group.

1. Luke says that the disciples were "restrained from recognizing him." What do you think some of these restraints might have been?

2. What keeps you from recognizing Jesus "on the way"?

3. How did the disciples come to recognize him?

4. How were the disciples transformed by their awareness that Jesus was risen?

5. How are you transformed by your faith in the resurrection?

There may be more questions than the participants can share in the remaining time. Questions 2 and 5 are most helpful in focusing their attention on their own faith and experience.

CLOSING PRAYER

Time: 10 minutes

Preparation
The leader will need to provide enough bread (a roll or loaf, not a slice) for each to receive some.

Song

"Are Not Our Hearts Burning Within Us?" or some familiar Easter hymn.

A Call to Remember

Leader:
"The Easter appearances of Jesus are the primary way in which the disciples came to know that Jesus was raised." Jesus lives! St. Paul never saw the empty tomb, yet he did experience the risen Lord on the road to Damascus. Paul believed that once we have experienced Jesus as alive, risen, Lord, we will be transformed and sent as apostles. Let us listen to Paul:

> *Reader:*
> A reading from St. Paul's first letter to the Corinthians (from 1 Cor 15:4-10).

Christ was raised on the third day in accordance with the Scriptures. He appeared to Cephas, then to the Twelve. After that he appeared to more than five hundred of us all at once, most of whom are still living. . . . After that he appeared to James, then to all the apostles. Last of all, as to one born out of time, he appeared to me. I am the least of the apostles . . . but by the grace of God, I am who I am.

> This is the word of the Lord.

> *All:*
> Thanks be to God!

Leader:
Like Paul, we never saw the empty tomb, but we can know, we can experience Jesus as certainly as Paul did. Jesus lives! Luke believed that once we have experienced that Jesus is alive, once we have met the risen Lord along our way and have recognized him, our hearts will be on fire to witness to him. Let us respond to this good news of his risen life among us and within us by praying this New Testament litany:

Litany

> *Reader:*
> We recognized him in the breaking of the bread (Lk 24:35).

(Leader silently breaks the roll or loaf in half and leaves it in the center of the group.)

All:

All I want is to know him and the power flowing from his resurrection (Phil 3:10).

Reader:

This is eternal life, risen life right now: to know you, the one true God and the one whom you sent, Jesus Christ (Jn 17:3).

All:

All I want is to know him and the power flowing from his resurrection.

Reader:

He is the wisdom of God and the power of God (1 Cor 1:24).

All:

All I want is to know him and the power flowing from his resurrection.

Reader:

Our Father and Mother who art in heaven, hallowed be thy name.

All:

All I want is to know him and the power flowing from his resurrection.

Reader:

Give us this day our daily bread.

(Leader breaks the bread into individual pieces and passes it so that each one may take and eat a piece.)

All:

All I want is to know him and the power flowing from his resurrection.

Reader:

And lead us not into temptation, but deliver us from evil, for the kingdom, the power and the glory are yours, now and forever. Amen.

All:
All I want is to know him and the power flowing from his resurrection.

(The leader now breaks the rest of the bread and gives some to each one. When everyone has finished eating, continue.)

Leader:
Let us go in peace to love and serve the risen Lord, Jesus!

All:
Thanks be to God!

Concluding Song

The same as the opening song—or perhaps a rousing Alleluia, or a well known Easter hymn.

FOLLOW-UP

A. Journaling

In the conclusion of John's gospel it says that "Jesus performed many other signs—signs not recorded here—in the presence of his disciples. But these have been recorded to help you believe that Jesus is the Messiah, the Son of God, so that through this faith you might have life in his name" (Jn 20:30-31).

List as many words as you can which are images of the resurrection to you.

List as many words as you can that are images of death to you.

How many of these words are connected with events in your life?

How many of these words are connected with people in your life?

What relationships, events, people are life-giving for you?

When have you experienced a death that has led to new life?

How has faith given you "life in his name"?

When Thomas saw the risen Lord he said, "My Lord and my God!" During the Eucharist we proclaim, "Christ has died, Christ is risen, Christ will come again!" Write your own personal affirmation of faith in the risen Lord.

B. Additional Resources

1. Read: Anthony Marinelli, *Understanding the Gospels,* Chapter 6, "The Death and Resurrection of Jesus," pp. 94-109.

2. Read: Raymond E. Brown, S.S., *Responses to 101 Questions on the Bible,* Questions 52-53.

3. Read: *The Catholic Study Bible,* commentary on the resurrection narratives, RG 404, 416, 435, 448.

4. Using the Hammond *Atlas of the Bible Lands,* find the places referred to in these passages: Mark 16:7; Matthew 28:10; Luke 24:13,33,50; John 21:1.

C. Further Reading

The New Jerome Biblical Commentary, "The Resurrection of Jesus," 81:120-134; "The Resurrection," 78:57.

Philip A. Cunningham, *Jesus and the Evangelists,* "The Resurrection and the Messianic Age," pp. 190-205.

5. The Beginnings of Christology

Preparation

- Read Perkins, Chapter 6, "The Beginnings of Christology."
- Read the following New Testament texts: Philippians 2:6-11, 1 Corinthians 8:6, 1 Corinthians 15:15-20, John 1:1-18.
- Reflect on the FOCUS statement and the REVIEW OF CONTENTS questions.

General Goals:
— That participants understand and appreciate the background, meaning and purpose of the titles and hymns applied to Jesus by the early Christians.
— That participants understand that the recognition of Jesus' identity as God was a slow and gradual process of growth in understanding for the first Christians.
— That participants engage in a process of reflection on their own christologies.

FOCUS

What we find in the New Testament is an expression of faith. The first Christians experienced the love, mercy and forgiveness of God when they encountered Jesus. The New Testament is about their struggle to put that experience into words. Before they wrote about it, or even told a comprehensive story, they first celebrated their experience in prayer and worship. Stories about Jesus were handed on in the context of the liturgy. They also attributed titles to Jesus. Some of these were Messiah, Son of Man, and Lord. Such titles carried a rich meaning from the Old Testament. The first Christians used these titles to name who Jesus was from their experience. This was the beginning of what theologians today call christology: the study of the identity and role of Jesus.

OPENING PRAYER

Time: 5 minutes

Preparation
Arrange a centerpiece consisting of a bowl of oil and a bowl of dirt. The oil may be cooking oil and need not fill the bowl. Clear matching bowls would be best. This centerpiece should also be used for the Closing Prayer.

Opening Song

Any song that uses some of the titles of Christ, perhaps a Lamb of God chant which allows for various titles to be inserted.

Leader:
Let us pray . . .

(Pause)
Lord Jesus, we believe that you are fully human, that you have put a body on God's unconditional and faithful love for us. We worship you as Lord, divine and unique Son of God. Pray with us as we praise God together in the words of Psalm 89.

Psalm 89

Right side:
Happy are we who walk in the light of your face, O Lord,
for kindness and truth go before you.
At your name we rejoice all the day,
for you have given us our King.

Left side:
Once you spoke to us, and to your faithful ones you said:
On a champion I have placed my crown;
I have found my servant and anointed him with holy oil.
My hand is always with him, my arm makes him strong.
My faithfulness and kindness shall be with him.

Right side:
He shall say of me:
"You are my father, my God, the rock, my savior."
I will make him first born, highest of the kings of the
      earth.

Left side:
Forever I will maintain my kindness toward him,
and my covenant with him stands firm.

Concluding Song

Repeat the song from the beginning or sing the refrain to "Psalm 89."

REVIEW OF CONTENTS

Objectives: That participants show, through their contribution to general group discussion, that they have a basic familiarity with the following concepts from the preparatory reading: the meaning of the term, christology, and the nature of the New Testament christologies; some of the ways the New Testament understood the resurrected or exalted Jesus; and the meaning and general origin of some of the major titles and hymns found in the New Testament.

Time: 25 minutes

1. What is christology? How does the christology of today's theologians differ from that of the New Testament authors? (See Perkins, pp. 110 and 112.)

Christology is a topic in Christian theology that deals with explanations of who Jesus is and what his relationship to God is. In the New Testament, however, we do not find systematic and abstract explanations. Rather, what we have are the beginnings of a process in the explanation of Jesus' identity and role. Images, titles, hymns and stories are used to try and express a developing notion of who Jesus is.

2. The christology that we find in the New Testament is greatly affected by the early Christians' experience of the resurrection of Jesus. (See Perkins, pp. 100-101, and the biblical texts to which she refers.)

a. What divine functions are attributed to the exalted Jesus?

Divine functions, some of which were originally attributed to angels (Dan 7:14-15 and 12:1), such as heavenly rule, judgment, salvation, acting as an agent of divine assistance in guiding and protecting the new community, were applied to the exalted Jesus.

b. How is the role of the exalted Jesus seen to be like that of the angels in Daniel 7:14-15?

This passage speaks of an "angelic figure in human form" ascending to the divine throne; Jesus was seen to have been exalted to a heavenly role after his death.

c. How is Jesus' role seen to differ from that of the angels? (Check Hebrews 1 which contains Old Testament references supporting the idea that Jesus is ''far superior to'' and possesses a relationship with God beyond that of any of the angels.)

God has addressed to Jesus such words as "You are my son . . ." ". . . anointed with the oil of gladness above your fellow kings," and ". . . your years will have no end." God has never addressed such words to the angels, who are "ministering spirits, sent to serve those who are to inherit salvation" (vs.14).

3. In attempting to express who they understood Jesus to be, the first Christians used titles that were available to them mainly from the Jewish Scriptures.

a. What were some of the associated meanings of the following titles that were applied to Jesus? (Summarized by Perkins, pp. 101-106.)

The emphasis here should be mainly on a recognition of the idea that the particular way in which the first Christians understood and spoke about Jesus reflects the categories for such understanding that were available to them. Detailed knowledge of the nuances of use of the titles at different historical times, for example, is not necessary.

i. Messiah (or Christ) (see also 2 Sam 23:1-17).

Messiah means "anointed one." The reference to 2 Samuel here contains mention of David as the "anointed one." The Jewish tradition contains references to the coming of "an anointed one" in the last days. It does not indicate whether that "anointed one" would be a prophet, priest, or king. An important factor in applying this title to Jesus was the expectation that the anointed one would initiate a new covenant with the righteous of Israel, hence establishing a new people.

ii. Son of Man (see also Dan 7).

There is little mention of this title (especially as *the* "Son of Man") in the Hebrew Scriptures. In the gospels it seems to be associated with the position of Jesus on the heavenly throne and his role in final judgment. This imagery is contained in the tradition, in Daniel 7 for example, and in 1 Enoch. Some scholars, as Perkins points out, link the meaning to the suffering servant theme. Jesus refers to himself as "son of man." The most probable development, Perkins suggests, was that it was first used as a generic term and later associated with meanings from the tradition suggested by events in Jesus' life, such as his passion interpreted as "messianic suffering."

iii. Son of God (see also Ps 2:7).

There is no conclusive evidence in the New Testament that this title referred to Jesus' divinity. The title had been used to refer to angels, the people of Israel, the king, or a righteous person. In referring to Jesus, the title seems to indicate a special relationship of Jesus to God. It expresses the idea of being specially chosen by God, as the people of Israel had been. The title was also applied to Christians (Rom 8:14-17).

iv. Lord.

This title was used to express the relationship of Christians to the exalted Jesus. It suggests divine status for Jesus, since the Israelites had applied this title to God. In the Greek tradition, it referred to gods and goddesses. It was also used to refer to human masters, however.

> b. Why did the suffering and death of Jesus present a problem in understanding Jesus as Messiah? (Perkins, p. 102)

The understandings of these titles inherited from the tradition did not obviously carry the expectation that the Messiah or the Son of God would suffer and die. The messianic ruler was to bring an end to suffering and death. It was only in the light of the resurrection that the first Christians could justify the sufferings of the "anointed one." The "son of man" title may in fact have been used to help justify the suffering and death of Jesus.

> c. How did the Jewish Christians deal with the problem of distinguishing Jesus (as Lord) from God (as Lord)? Why did the early Christians rarely speak of Jesus as God? (See pages 106 and 109 of Perkins.)

The early Christians distinguished Jesus as Lord from God as Lord by referring to Jesus as a divine agent of God. They also used the language of Father and Son to preserve this distinction. The strong belief in monotheism influenced the early Christians in this distinction. The New Testament contains evidence that the first Christians were careful to refute any charges of blasphemy (Jn 5:18-29). Perkins observes that it took several centuries for Christians to be able to express Jesus' divinity in a way that protected belief in one God.

> 4. What do scholars believe is the origin of the hymns, such as Philippians 2:6-11, that are incorporated into the New Testament? (Perkins discusses this on p. 107.)

It seems clear from the earliest New Testament writings that worship was the context in which the first Christians first expressed their faith in Jesus. So the titles were used first in liturgical formulas, and eventually in longer forms such as hymns. These are incorporated by the New Testament authors because they contain ways in which the early Christians expressed the uniqueness of Jesus.

VIDEO

Objective: To help participants understand the process by which the early Church came to formulate its understanding of Jesus.

Time: 20 minutes

New Testament Christologies

As you view this video, please make note of the following:

1. What is christology? _____

_____

2. What do the following titles of Jesus mean in the New Testament? Note that these meanings are not necessarily the same as those they have acquired in the subsequent evolution of the Church's faith.

a. Christ _____

b. Lord _____

c. Son of God _____

Video Outline

New Testament Christologies

1. "Who do you say that I am?"
   a. interviews
   b. christology as the way we answer the question, "Who do you say that I am?"
   c. plurality of christologies: examples from art

2. The process of forming a christology
   a. pluralism of christologies in the New Testament: four gospels
   b. the gradual process of clarifying belief in Jesus

3. New Testament christology: Jesus for us
   a. Christ: not the triumphant messiah but the suffering messiah
   b. Lord: not the same as the Father, but the one who, because of his obedience, has been exalted (Phil 2:6-11)
   c. Son of God: not the second person of the Trinity, but the one in a unique relationship with God (Heb 1:5-13)

BREAK

(10 minutes)

LEARNING ACTIVITY

Objectives: That participants understand that there is New Testament evidence of a process of struggle on the part of Jesus' contemporaries and early followers to understand and express who they experienced him to be. That they understand what some of this evidence actually says about who Jesus is.

Time: 25 minutes

This is a group exercise. Set up groups of no more than five to allow for maximum participation by everyone. If necessary, more than one group can work on each of the hymns. In introducing the exercise, emphasize the fact that what is being uncovered in this work with the Scriptures is not just content, i.e., who did the first Christians understand Jesus to be, but a process by which they came to that understanding. It is also important to stress the fact that our present understanding of Jesus, while based on the New Testament formulations, has been clarified and systematized. We should not try to force these later developments onto the New Testament texts.

This exercise will examine two of the christological hymns of the first Christians. You will be asked to take a more detailed look at some of the references to experiences of Jesus and/or Old Testament ideas and images used by the first Christians in trying to express their understanding of Jesus. It is hoped that by doing so you will come to a greater appreciation of the process by which christology developed and of some of the earliest explanations of who Jesus was and of his mission in this world.

Group A

Read carefully Philippians 2:6-11. (Perkins quotes this passage on pp. 107-108.) Then discuss the following questions. Record your answers. Using the textbook to read this passage leaves Bibles free for locating the other passages more conveniently.

1. At the beginning of this hymn, there is a hint of Jesus' special relationship to God: "He was in the form of God." Check 1 Corinthians 8:6. How is Jesus described in this passage?

Jesus is described as "one Lord Jesus Christ" with a role very close to that of God the Father. Jesus was the one *in* whom all things were made and *through* whom we live; everything came *from* God *for* whom we live. Care is taken here not to multiply gods by making Jesus also a god.

Compare this description of Jesus to the role of the "wisdom" of God in Wisdom 9:9 and Proverbs 3:19.

Wisdom is spoken of in these passages as being present when God made the world and it was "by wisdom" that the Lord founded the world. This is suggestive of the role given to Jesus in the Corinthians passage above.

2. Read the references to Adam and Eve in Genesis 2:15-17 and 3:22-24. How is Jesus contrasted with Adam and Eve in the hymn in Philippians 2?

Jesus is contrasted with Adam and Eve in that he, unlike them, does not try to be like God, is obedient to God's commands, and is without sin.

3. Summarize the following references to Jesus and obedience in the gospels.
a. Matthew 26:39, 42
b. John 4:34, 5:30, 6:38
c. Mark 3:35
d. Matthew 7:21

a. This is Jesus' acceptance of the Father's will in reference to his coming passion and death, despite Jesus' human desire not to suffer.

b. These passages contain three assertions of Jesus that his mission is to do the will of his Father.

c. Jesus states that whoever does the will of his Father is mother and sister and brother to him.

d. Only those who do the will of the Father will enter the kingdom; crying out "Lord, Lord!" will not suffice.

4. Jesus was without sin (see 2 Cor 5:21). Therefore, his death could not be seen as a punishment for sin. However, crucifixion was a scandal in first-century Judaism. Only the worst criminals suffered crucifixion. According to this hymn, how did the first Christians come to understand and explain Jesus' death?

Jesus' death is given significance in that it showed forth the extent of Jesus' humility (in taking on real humanness) and of his obedience to the will of his father.

5. Read Isaiah 52:13-15 and 53:12. How does this help us to understand the meaning of the phrases, "humbling himself" and "being exalted" in the Philippians hymn?

These passages connect the suffering and humiliated servant of God with the reward of exaltation. The passage in 53:12 also relates surrendering to death with "taking away sins" and winning pardon for many.

6. Use your own words to compose a brief (five or six sentences) summary of what the first Christians were saying about Jesus in this hymn. Someone should be prepared to read this summary to the large group.

Look for mention of the following understandings of Jesus: Jesus did not desire or seek equality with God, he was humble and obedient, he was truly human, he willingly accepted death, and, like the servant of God in Isaiah, by that death was exalted by God and won salvation for all. Jesus is contrasted with Adam and Eve and likened to the suffering servant in Isaiah. It would be helpful to re-emphasize here that this hymn contains indications of how the first Christians experienced Jesus, i.e., as humble and obedient, even in suffering and death, yet as overcoming death by his resurrection. The references to the Scriptures and the interpretations of these references is in light of these experiences. For the sake of time, if more than one group has done the same exercise, you may want to either have all the summaries of this exercise read first and then comment; or hear just one, and make general comments on that summary for the benefit of all.

Group B

Read carefully Colossians 1:15-20. Discuss and record your answers to the following questions.

1. How is Jesus the "image of the invisible God"? See John 1:18.

John suggests that it is in Jesus that we see God. No one has actually seen God, but (by implication) we have seen the Son, who reveals God.

2. Jesus is described as the "first-born" of God. What do the following Old Testament references say about God's first-born? To whom does each passage refer?
a. Psalm 89:27-28
b. Exodus 4:22-23
c. Proverbs 8:22-31

a. The first-born will be made the highest of the earthly kings. The passage refers to David.

b. The first-born of God is to be free to serve God; the text is referring to the chosen people, Israel.

c. The first-born is begotten of God before anything else was created and was present when the world was created. The reference in verse 30 to the role of first born as craftsman suggests a role for Wisdom in the creation itself. The passage is referring to Wisdom (see vs. 12).

How does Christ's place as "first-born" differ from those described in the first two passages above?

Christ is above not only kings, but all creatures and all creation. In him all was created; his status is exalted above that of service to God as well.

How does Christ's role compare to the Wisdom of God as "first-born" described in Proverbs 8?

The role ascribed to Christ in the hymn seems to reflect the role of Wisdom as described in Proverbs 8. Both are given precedence over all of creation and all creatures. Christ is also seen to have a role in creation (all things are created *in* him). Wisdom is compared to a craftsman.

3. a. What is Jesus' relationship to the angels (thrones, dominations, principalities, and powers), according to this hymn?

Jesus is seen to be above all the angels and preceding them in existence
as well.

> b. What does Ephesians 1:20-21 say about Jesus' relation-
> ship to the angels?

This passage also asserts that Jesus is higher than the angels and any
name present or to come.

> 4. a. How are the church and Jesus related? (Read also
> Rom 12:3-8.)

Jesus is head of the church. Romans 12 states that we, the members of
the church, are one body in Christ.

> b. What does this relationship imply about how Jesus will
> continue to be in the world?

Jesus will continue to be present in the world in the church, the members
of which will continue his mission, the building of the kingdom.

> 5. Jesus is also a reconciler through his death on the
> cross, according to this hymn. Read Ephesians 2:11-21.
> Describe the example of ''reconciliation in Christ'' that is
> given here.

The Gentiles are now also chosen. They are part of the body of Christ,
the church. They are reconciled through Christ.

> 6. Compose a brief (five or six sentences) summary of
> what the first Christians who prayed or sang this hymn
> were expressing about who Jesus was. Someone should
> be prepared to read the summary to the larger group.

Look for the following understandings of Jesus: Jesus has a special relationship with God, even closer than that of the angels; he was present
at and played a role in creation; he is head of all the world and in a special way of the church, his body on earth; he is also a reconciler. See also
the emphasis suggested in commenting on the summary for Group A.

FAITH SHARING

Objective: That participants become aware of their own expressions of who Jesus is for them and by examining these expressions increase their awareness of their own christology, who they understand Jesus to be.

Time: 25 minutes

Participants should be asked to work alone on this exercise and then be invited to share their reflections with the rest of the group. Again, if the group is large, sharing could be done with partners, or in small groups of seven or less.

1. Make a list of the titles of Jesus that have most meaning for you, or that you commonly use in addressing Jesus. These do not have to be biblical titles.

2. Is there a prayer or hymn (liturgical or personal) that best expresses who Jesus is for you? Make a note of it.

3. Why do these titles, prayers, and/or hymns appeal to you? What aspects of your understanding of Jesus do they express?

You will be invited to share your reflections with the group.

CLOSING PRAYER

Time: 10 minutes

Song

A song that uses the name or titles of Jesus, such as Carey Landry's "Brother Jesus" or "Song of the Transfiguration."

A Call to Remember

Leader:
"The New Testament is an expression of faith," that is, a trust in Jesus in whom the first Christians "experienced the love, mercy, and forgiveness of God." The love and mercy of God is named in the Jewish Scriptures and is sung about in Psalm 89, our opening prayer. God's unconditional and tender love is *hesed* in Hebrew, and God's faithfulness is *'emit.* Jesus has put a body on God's kindness and fidelity.

Reader:
A reading from the book of Exodus (34:6) . . .

The Lord passed in front of Moses and cried out: "The Lord, the Lord, a merciful and gracious God, slow to anger and rich in kindness and fidelity, in *hesed* and *'emit.*"

This is the word of the Lord.

All:
Thanks be to God!

Leader:
Jesus is characterized not only by kindness and faithfulness on our behalf, but by humility and obedience in his relationship with God. Our session has focused on Jesus' special relationship to God as the anointed. Our symbols for contemplation are a bowl of oil and a bowl of dirt. The Spirit of the Lord anointed him. This is symbolized by oil. He is totally human. This is symbolized by the dirt, which in Latin is *humus,* earth. This is the root of our English words human and humility.

Jesus is obedient. Obedience does not mean conformity, but comes from the Latin word for listening. Jesus listened for the Spirit of God in his life, heard the good news of God's love for us, preached it and would not take it back even when threatened with death. God wills that we should know how faithfully and mercifully God loves us. God willed that Jesus should be faithful to this truth which he embodied. But God did not will that Jesus be betrayed, tortured and killed. God willed that Jesus be like us in all things, a creature of the earth: limited, mortal. And so Jesus suffered like us and died like the most outcast of us.

His humility does not mean that he puts himself down, but that he admits that he is human, accepting of our of earthiness with its limits, weakness and death. In becoming fully human, "even to death on a cross," he became fully alive. St. Irenaeus wrote, "The human being fully alive is the glory of God."

Let us ponder these things for a few moments in our hearts. Pause for a few moments of silence.

A Call to Respond

Leader:
Let us respond to this good news with this New Testament hymn from John's gospel which celebrates the *hesed* and *'emit* of God, translated here as the grace and truth of God, taking our human flesh.

Right side:
He came to his own . . . and to those who did accept him he gave the power to become the children of God.

Left side:
The Word became flesh and dwelt among us.

Right side:
We have seen his glory, the glory of the Father's only Son, full of grace and truth, full of *hesed* and *'emit.*

Left side:
Out of his fullness we have all received grace upon grace upon grace upon grace.

Right side:
The law was given through Moses, but grace and truth, *hesed* and *'emit,* have come through Jesus Christ.

Left side:
No one has ever seen God, but the one who is closest to the Father's heart has made God known.

Leader:
Now let us join Jesus in his prayer.

All:
Our Father and Mother, who art in heaven . . .
for the kingdom, the power and the glory are yours now
and forever.

Leader:
Let the glory and power be yours, our God. Let the glory
you take in us flow from our being fully human, ever
more and more alive to all that is of the earth. We thank
you for Jesus, for his kindness and fidelity, for his obedience and humility, and especially for his being human,
like us in all things. We pray in his name and in the power of the Holy Spirit.

All:
Amen.

Leader:
Let us now go to love and serve the Lord and glorify God
in all that we do.

All:
Thanks be to God!

Concluding Song

Perhaps the same as the opening song or a recording of the "Hallelujah
Chorus" from Handel's *Messiah*.

REMINDER FOR NEXT WEEK:
You are invited to share something of your own image of
Christ from your journal next session. Consider making
up your own christological hymn, or paint, draw, com-
pose music, or select art or music that speaks to you of
Christ. We will begin our next session with this sharing.

FOLLOW-UP

A. Journaling

Think about how you have experienced Jesus in your life. Which roles of Jesus seem to have most meaning for you? Does the exaltation of Jesus, his presence from the beginning of creation, his headship of the church, for example, have any meaning for you? Do you have favorite artistic representations of Jesus (pictures, statues)? Which aspects of Jesus' life, death and resurrection are expressed in those?

Write your own christological hymn or prayer on the basis of these reflections. (You may want to represent your ideas in drawing, painting or music.)

B. Additional Resources

1. Here are some other prayers and hymns found in the New Testament to read and reflect on:

> Luke 1:46-55 (The Magnificat)
> Luke 1:68-79 (The Benedictus)
> Luke 2:29-32
> Colossians 1:15-20
> Ephesians 1:3-10
> 1 Peter 1:3-9
> Acts 4:23-31 (community prayer)

2. Read: Anthony Marinelli, *Understanding the Gospels,* "Titles of Christ in the Synoptic Gospels," pp. 58-59.

3. Read: Raymond E. Brown, S.S., *Responses to 101 Questions on the Bible,* Questions 69-76.

4. Using the Hammond *Atlas of the Bible Lands,* locate the following places which are associated with the Scriptures studied in the session: Caeserea Philippi, Philippi, Corinth, Colossae, Ephesus.

C. Further Reading

The New Jerome Biblical Commentary, "The Identity of Jesus," 78:29-43; "Development in the New Testament Understanding of Jesus," 81:12-24.

John F. O'Grady, *The Four Gospels and the Jesus Tradition,* "The Jesus Tradition," pp. 7-24.

6. Mark: Jesus, Suffering Servant

Preparation

- Read Perkins, Chapter 12, "Mark: Jesus, Suffering Servant."
- Read Mark 2:1-3:6 and 8:22-10:52.
- Reflect on the FOCUS statement and the REVIEW OF CONTENTS questions.

General Goals:
— To lead participants in an appreciation of the link which Mark's gospel establishes between suffering and discipleship.
— To reflect on the relevance of Mark's vision of discipleship for today.

FOCUS

One of the major themes of Mark's gospel is that Jesus, the powerful savior, saves not by an assertion of divine or human power, but through his suffering. Likewise, his disciples will be called upon to suffer. Mark's gospel seems to be addressed to a suffering community. Peter has been martyred (ca. A.D. 64) and the community faces misunderstanding and rejection. There is an apparent need to deal with the relevance and meaning of this suffering in the light of the Christian mission.

OPENING PRAYER

Time: 5 minutes

Preparation
As the participants assemble, send them into small groups of three or four.
If some have forgotten their journal material about Christ, those could be
fifth or sixth members of a small group. Plan for only three or four sharings, per group, however, or this will take too much time. Have soft music
playing as people assemble and wait.

Leader:
Grace and peace be with you.

All:
And also with you!

Leader:
We are assembled in small groups so that we might share
personally some of what Christ means to us. Our listening
and receiving each other without judging is a kind of contemplation. To empty our heads and hearts of the many
voices we bring here and in order to be more open to
receive, let us now close our eyes and breathe deeply . . .

(After 30-40 seconds) Breathe out all your worries tonight.

(Leave 20-30 seconds) Breathe out the frustrations of today.

(20-30 seconds) Breathe in the peace of God.

(20-30 seconds) Breathe in the love of God.

(20-30 seconds) Now, let us begin our sharing . . .

As the leader notices that one or two groups have finished, those groups
could softly begin to sing "Peace Is Flowing Like a River," or an alleluia—
something known without books to everyone. Other groups will join in as
they finish.

Song

"Peace is Flowing Like a River" or an alleluia

REVIEW OF CONTENTS

Objectives: To reinforce familiarity with Mark's understanding of what a gospel is and with some of the features of Mark's gospel.

Time: 25 minutes

Recall and briefly write in the spaces provided your response to each of the following questions. References to the Perkins text and to the gospel of Mark are provided where appropriate for easy review. Be prepared to share your responses with the group and to support them when called upon by your program leader.

Point out to the participants that the exercise follows the first part of Perkins, Chapter 12, "The Composition of Mark" and some of the gospel passages suggested there.

1. Make a list of five or six words or phrases that indicate what you understood the word ''gospel'' to mean prior to the reading for this session (or to this course).

It is likely that many of the participants will have thought of "gospel" merely as a book of the New Testament or as part of the Liturgy of the Word. The purpose here is to focus on the deeper meaning given to the word in the New Testament, as well as to see how with Mark's writing we first get a unique kind of text which we recognize by the name "gospel."

2. What seems to be the original meaning of the word ''gospel'' as used by New Testament writers? (St. Paul's use—Perkins, p. 203).

The message of salvation which Paul preaches. The word has its origin in a verb meaning "to bring or announce good news," as in Isaiah, who brought good news to the Israelites in captivity.

3. What meaning does Mark give the word ''gospel,'' in each of the following passages:

a. Mark 1:14-15
b. Mark 8:35, 10:29, 13:10, 14:9
c. Mark 14:9

What does Perkins suggest is the meaning of this last passage?

a. The preaching of Jesus that the reign of God is at hand.

b. Jesus himself, as well as the preaching about him is good news.

c. The gospel is something more than sayings and stories about Jesus. There may have been a written collection of stories and sayings about Jesus in existence before Mark's gospel was written. Mark would have used these as sources for his own gospel.

4. How does Mark's use of the word "gospel" compare to your understanding of the word expressed in number 1, above?

Emphasize the connection of the word "gospel" to the actual reign of God initiated by Jesus.

5. What does Perkins say is the theme of Mark's gospel? What events make up the center of the plot (p. 205)?

The truth of Jesus is found only on the cross. The center of the plot includes Peter's profession of faith in Jesus as Messiah, Jesus' prediction of his passion and his rebuke of Peter for a promise of faithfulness he will not keep, and the prediction by Jesus that his followers will also suffer (Mk 8).

6. What is meant by the "messianic secret" in Mark? To what paradox does it point? (See Perkins, p. 205, Mk 1:40-45, 8:27-30, 9:9.)

The command of Jesus to his followers or to those he heals is to keep silent about his teachings and miracles. It points to the paradox that the all-powerful Son of God will save us by death on a cross, the greatest fact and symbol of human frailty.

The connection is made in Mark 8. Jesus commands Peter to silence after Peter recognizes him as Messiah. What follows is an explanation by Jesus that his role as Messiah will be achieved through suffering and death.

VIDEO

Objective: That participants be more aware of the kind of community out of which Mark composed his gospel, and the effect this had on how the message and mission of Jesus is presented.

Time: 20 minutes

The Cross in the Gospel of Mark

As you view this video, please make note of the following:

1. What were some of the special concerns facing Mark's audience?

_____

_____

2. Why does Peter argue with Jesus?

_____

_____

3. How do the other apostles respond to Jesus' message of the cross?

_____

_____

Video Outline

The Cross in the Gospel of Mark

1. The paradox of the cross

2. The Markan community
   a. probably Rome, experiencing persecution
   b. Mark seeks to interpret the suffering

3. The Markan Jesus
   a. a hidden Messiah
   b. a suffering Messiah

4. Peter, mirror of the community
   a. the centrality of the cross
   b. the difficulty of accepting it

5. The cross in contemporary Christian communities
   a. Solentiname

BREAK

(10 minutes)

LEARNING ACTIVITY

Objectives: That the participants practice an attentive reading of the gospel text, become familiar with the demands of discipleship expressed there, and recognize the humanness of the first followers of Jesus and their struggle to be true disciples.

Time: 25 minutes

By now, the routine for division into groups is probably well established. The groups should be no larger than five persons to allow maximum involvement by all. Two or more groups may work on the same exercise, if necessary. It may be helpful to continue to stress the necessity of everyone's involvement, the importance of listening to the word of God, whether read silently or proclaimed by one of the members, and the necessity of listening to one another. Most of the gospel readings are quite familiar to most of us; active listening, however, can reveal dimensions we had not noticed before. If possible, (if there is ample space between groups) have a volunteer read the assigned gospel passage aloud for the rest of the group.

At the end of the small group activity, you may want to ask if there are any questions or difficulties regarding questions 1 and 2. Then ask for the responses to question 3 in each group. Record the characteristics of discipleship on a chalk board, newsprint, or poster paper. Watch for misreading or the projection of preconceived notions about discipleship onto the text. That is the purpose of asking each group to support their findings with verses from the assigned passages. Have all the participants record the characteristics of all the groups.

Divide into three (or more) groups as directed by your leader. Briefly make notes in the spaces provided as you research and discuss the questions related to one of the following passages (or set of passages) from Mark's gospel. Each group will be asked to contribute to an outline portrait of discipleship as presented by Mark (your responses to question 3) at the end of the activity.

Group 1

Read Mark 4.

1. Are there any clues here as to what Jesus' disciples were like? (Check verses 13 and 40-41, for example.)

v. 13—Jesus accused his disciples of not understanding the parable he just told. By implication, how will they understand everything else connected with his mission?

vs. 40-41—The disciples are "terrified," filled with awe. Jesus accuses them of lacking faith; by their own question (vs. 41) they admit no knowledge of who he is.

2. What images are used to describe the reign of God (see vs. 26-29 and 30-32)? Explain what these images tell us about what the reign of God is like.

The images used are the growth from sowing of seed to harvest time of a corn field, and the growth of a mustard seed.

The reign of God grows silently, without our full knowledge of exactly how it is happening, until we recognize its full presence (vs. 26-29). The reign of God also starts very small; in the beginning it looks very insignificant and fragile, smaller than any other kingdom or worldly institution. In the end, however, it becomes the largest kingdom of all.

3. Make a list of the characteristics of a true disciple as these are revealed in the chapter of Mark. Note the verses that support your answer.

The suggested answers below are not the only possible ones, or the only way of expressing the same idea.

Characteristic of discipleship	Supporting verses
listens attentively to the Word, is nourished by it and acts on it	vs. 20
gives witness to one's faith	vs. 21
is giving	vs. 22
is patient and trusting	implication of vs. 26-29 and 30-32
has faith and calm trust	vs. 40-41

Group 2

Read Mark 10:13-45.

1. What words and phrases are used in this passage to describe the attitudes and behaviors of Jesus' followers? (Check verses 13, 24-26, 32, and 35-37.) Do you think they were really aware of the true nature of Jesus' mission and of the reign of God? Explain.

vs. 13—disciples scold those who are bringing children to Jesus.

vs. 24-26—disciples "marvel" and are "overwhelmed" by the words of Jesus regarding how difficult it will be for the rich to enter heaven.

vs. 32—wonderment of disciples, fear of followers.

vs. 35-37—James and John request to sit one at the right and one at the left of Jesus when he enters his kingdom.

These passages point out the fact that in Mark's gospel the disciples and followers of Jesus are often in awe of him, but show no real understanding of his mission or of the nature of the kingdom he is establishing. Verses like 42-45 are clear indications that they are not aware of the "overturning" of values that happens with Jesus. Hence, his response that, unlike the kind of authority exercised among the Gentiles, his authority rests on service. The ordinary norms of this world do not apply.

2. With what words of Jesus does Mark express what is expected of a true disciple? Are there any words of encouragement or hope? If so, what are they?

One must accept the reign of God "like a little child" (vs. 15); go beyond obeying the commandments to giving all—"sell all you have and give it to the poor" (vs. 21); serve others—"whoever wants to be first, must serve the needs of all" (vs. 44).

Words of encouragement and hope include Jesus' claim that his kingdom belongs to the "little ones" of this world—children, child-like, the least among us. Verses 26-30 also contain Jesus' promises that even though it seems improbable that many will be saved, with God all things are possible. Ultimately, salvation is the gift of God.

Also, whoever has given all for the sake of Jesus and the gospel will receive a hundredfold in this life and, in the next, life everlasting. There is also the prophecy of the resurrection in verse 34. Life will triumph over death.

3. List the characteristics of the true disciple that are revealed in this passage. Support your answers by noting the verses to which you are referring.

Characteristic of discipleship	Supporting verses
trusting acceptance, simplicity	vs. 14-15
totally committed, giving all	vs. 21-22
relying on God	vs. 27
dedicated to service of others, detached from worldly honor	vs. 42-45

Group 3

Read Mark 1:14-20, 2:13-17, 13:9-13.

1. Summarize briefly the words and actions of Jesus and his disciples that show the urgency of becoming a disciple. (Check 1:14-15; 1:18; and 13:9). What impressions are given about the kind of kingdom Jesus has come to establish?

vs. 1:14-15—Jesus announces that the reign of God is at hand. In response, his followers must reform their lives and believe.

vs. 1:18—Simon and Andrew do not hesitate; they *immediately* leave their nets and follow Jesus when called.

vs. 13:9—The disciples must always be ready—God's reign is at hand.

The passages assigned here give the impression that the kingdom is more important than any worldly affairs (the first disciples drop their nets, Levi leaves his tax-collections). Sinners are welcomed; actually, they have some kind of priority. Jesus says he came to call sinners, not the righteous (2:17). A lot of suffering will be associated with the proclamation of the gospel and the coming of the kingdom. Jesus' disciples will be persecuted by the powers of this world. Steadfastness through all of this will mark those who will "come through safely," be members of the kingdom.

2. What does Jesus require of his disciples, those who will be members of his kingdom?

They should place highest value on the demands of discipleship; no worldly concern should stand in the way of their following him. They should go beyond the established bounds of social propriety (not eating with sinners) for the sake of the kingdom. They should be in constant readiness for the coming of the kingdom and be ready to endure all kinds of suffering to bring it about.

3. Make a list of the characteristics of discipleship revealed in these gospel passages. Note the verses which support your answers.

Characteristic of discipleship	Supporting verses
reformed life—one that in belief and action conforms to the gospel	vs. 1:15
no hesitation in responding to the call to discipleship	vs. 1:18, 20; 2:14
called by Jesus (not of one's own initiative)	vs. 1:17, 20; 2:14
vigilant	vs. 13:9
steadfast, willing to suffer, strong faith and commitment	vs. 13:9-13

(If not already dealt with, a brief reference to the worldview and apocalyptic that underlies Mark 13 may shed more light on this passage and its imagery and make it more understandable to the participants. See Perkins, p. 204, second paragraph. You may also refer those interested back to Perkins, Chapter 2, especially pp. 38-45.)

All groups:

As your leader collects the lists of characteristics of discipleship compiled by all the groups, copy the compilation below for future reference.

FAITH SHARING

Objective: To reflect on the relevance of discipleship as Mark presents it to Christian life today. To modern Christians, Mark's world may seem in many ways strange and distant. Yet, the concern to understand the relationship of salvation to suffering is always a relevant Christian concern.

Time: 25 minutes

Ask participants to reflect silently on these questions, jotting down notes to aid their reflection and memory (about 5 minutes). Then invite them to share their reflections on at least some of the questions. Try to ensure that everyone who wishes to will get a chance to speak to the group and that a few do not dominate the discussion. The purpose is not to prove one's own response, to be "more right," but to benefit from sharing in the faith life of others.

1. Reflect on the characteristics of a disciple as presented in Mark's gospel. Which of these characteristics do you think are especially valuable for Christians today? Choose one or two and explain your choice.

There are no right or wrong answers here. Concentrate on helping participants articulate the reasons for their choices. It is important to be sensitive to the personal experiences and concerns that may underlie these reasons.

2. Which characteristics do you think are the most difficult to acquire in today's world? Why?

Answers will most likely point to the consumerism in today's society, the many distractions, and the difficulty of giving priority to discipleship. There is no longer a sense of urgency in preparing for the immediate fulfillment of the kingdom. It could be pointed out, however, that there is an urgency surrounding issues such as establishing peace in many parts of the world, of sheltering the homeless, or of responding to other kinds of poverty, both spiritual and physical.

3. How can modern Christian disciples offer hope and support to one another? Is Mark's gospel helpful in this regard? Explain.

Mark's gospel shows that a precedent has been set by Jesus himself in showing the salvific character of suffering. Suffering, however, is not for its own sake, but for the sake of the reign of God. Prediction of suffering is followed by the promise of resurrection or of the reward of faithfulness.

82

CLOSING PRAYER

Time: 10 minutes

Preparation
The leader should prepare a centerpiece of just two bare branches, crossed.

A Call to Respond

Song

Any Lenten hymn from song books, on tape or on a record.

Leader:
"One of the major themes of Mark's gospel is that Jesus, the powerful Savior, saves not by an assertion of divine or human powerfulness, but through his suffering." He was weak, limited, annoyed, frustrated. His suffering was life-long, longer by far than the last few hours of his life. Jesus saves us by becoming like us. What is assumed by Jesus, the ancient fathers of the church taught, is saved. Why did Jesus fail? What does God want us to learn about failure and weakness as we contemplate the Suffering Servant?

Reading

Reader:
A reading from the gospel according to Mark (10:17-18, 21).

All:
Glory to you, O Lord.

Reader:
As Jesus was setting out on a journey, a man ran up, knelt down before him and asked: "Good teacher, what must I do to inherit eternal life?" Jesus answered him: "Why do you call me good? No one is good but God alone." Then Jesus, looking at him tenderly, said . . .

Leader:
Jesus looks at us tenderly. St. Teresa of Avila says that to contemplate, we simply look at Jesus looking at us, humbly and tenderly. Right now, look at Jesus looking at you tenderly.

(Allow a few moments for reflection.)

Litany

Leader:
Now we will look at him tenderly as we watch his suffering all through his life, suffering so very much like our own. Let us respond to these gospel sentences by praying: You are like us, Lord.

Reader:
When your solitude is spoiled (1:35-38),

All:
You are like us, Lord.

Reader:
When you are accused and harassed (2:7),

All:
You are like us, Lord.

Reader:
When you are angry and grieved (3:5),

All:
You are like us, Lord.

Reader:
When your family, even your mother, misunderstands you (3:21, 31),

All:
You are like us Lord.

Leader:
When the crowd laughs scornfully at you (5:40),

All:
You are like us Lord.

Leader:
When your neighbors reject you (6:3),

All:
You are like us Lord.

Leader:
When your heart aches with pity (6:34),

All:
You are like us Lord

Leader:
When your friends' hearts are hardened (6:52),

All:
You are like us Lord.

Leader:
When your vacation at the seashore of Tyre is interrupted (7:24),

All:
You are like us Lord.

Leader:
When you sigh from the depth of your spirit in frustration (8:12),

All:
You are like us Lord.

Leader:
When you are so infuriated you call your best friend a devil (8:33),

All:
You are like us Lord.

Leader:
When you become indignant with your friends (10:14),

All:
You are like us Lord.

Leader:
When your friends misunderstand, betray, fall asleep, deny and run away from you in your crisis time,

All:
You are like us, Lord.

Leader:
Let us pray.

All:
Lord Jesus, our brother and our friend, thank you for

being like us in everything, for knowing in your very body how painful our limits and weakness really are. Thank you for sharing life with us. We ask for the deepening of your Spirit within us so that we may grow more and more like you in everything, day by day. Unite us with one another and with all your church, your body which still suffers throughout the world. Look on us all tenderly as we keep our eyes fixed on you. We ask and praise and thank in your name. Amen.

Leader:
We continue to pray in Jesus' name:

All:
Our Father and Mother . . .
for the kingdom, the power and the glory are yours, now and forever. Amen.

Leader:
Let us go to love and serve our Suffering Servant and one another.

All:
Thanks be to God.

Concluding Song

Repeat the Lenten hymn which opened this prayer.

FOLLOW-UP

A. Journaling

In Mark's gospel, Jesus is almost always with his disciples. They are called at the outset of the gospel (Mk 1). Because of the inability of his disciples to understand, in most of what Jesus says and does, he is alone. They fall asleep while he suffers in Gethsemane and abandon him in his death. Even at the news of his resurrection, they flee in bewilderment and fear (Mk 16:8).

Read one or more of the following passages. In what incidents in your life do you identify with the solitary Jesus? When do you identify with the bewildered disciples? What are the sources of your strength in those times?

Mark 6:1-6—Jesus not accepted in his "own part of the country."

Mark 8:14-21—Disciples do not understand the multiplication of the loaves.

Mark 9:30-32—Disciples fail to understand the approaching death of Jesus.

Mark 14:32-42—Gethsemane.

Mark 14:43-52—Jesus is arrested.

Mark 14:66-72—Peter's denial of Jesus.

Additional Resources

1. Read over as much of Mark's gospel as time allows using the outline in Perkins, p. 206 as a guide.

2. If your Bible has an introduction to Mark's gospel, read it.

3. Read: Anthony Marinelli, *Understanding the Gospels*, Chapter 4, "The Synoptic Gospels," pp. 54-60.

4. Read: *The Catholic Study Bible*, "Mark," RG 405-417.

5. Scholars believe that Mark's audience was probably the Christian community in Rome. Using you Hammond *Atlas of the Bible Lands,* locate Rome.

Further Reading

The New Jerome Biblical Commentary, "The Gospel of Mark," Article 41.

Philip A. Cunningham, *Jesus and the Evangelists,* "The Marcan Jesus: Suffering Son of Man," pp. 26-45.

John F. O'Grady, *The Four Gospels and the Jesus Tradition,* "The Jesus Tradition and the Cross: Mark," pp. 25-78.

7. Matthew: Jesus, Teacher of Israel

Preparation
- Read Perkins, Chapter 13, "Matthew: Jesus, Teacher of Israel."
- Read the sermons in Matthew:

Matthew 5:1-7:29	Matthew 18:1-35
Matthew 9:35-11:1	Matthew 19:1-20:34
Matthew 13:1-53	Matthew 24:1-25:46

- Reflect on the FOCUS statement and the REVIEW OF CONTENTS questions.

General Goals:
- To enable participants to discover some of the major themes in Matthew's gospel and how Matthew's particular pastoral concerns help shape his selection and presentation of these themes.
- To help participants discover the relevance of Matthew's concerns for their experience of the church today.

FOCUS

Matthew's community is believed to have been made up primarily of Jewish Christians. By the time of the composition of his gospel, however, the community that believed in Jesus found itself outside the confines of Judaism. This led to many conflicts, both external and internal. The early Jewish Christians faced opposition and rejection by their former Jewish communities, but neither were they Gentiles. Matthew tries to offer an interpretation of their situation that encompasses both continuity with their past and an incorporation of the newness in Jesus' mission and message. Within the community, disagreements and friction were also present. The reign of God did not seem to produce perfection. Should not the Messiah have brought total peace and happiness? Many became discouraged; their faith grew cold. Matthew encourages his community to trust in the power of Jesus and his continued presence. He shows how the ambiguities will continue to exist while the reign of God is in this world, but at the end of time things will be different. Jesus' followers are to listen to Jesus' teaching, through which they will know how to be faithful disciples.

OPENING PRAYER

Time: 5 minutes

Preparation
Prepare a place where the Bible may lie open and "enthroned." Burn incense before it as people enter the room, and again for the Closing Prayer. If it is not possible to use incense, use a candle and/or a plant, or a cloth draped tastefully to set off this Bible as special tonight.

Song
"O Come, O Come Emmanuel!"

Reader:
Jesus fulfills the Old Law, completes it, makes it full. If the Jewish people discovered God in the Law, Christians discover God in Christ. God once expressed God's own self through the Law, but in our day, God expresses God in Jesus Christ (Heb 1:1).

Jesus is God-with-us, Emmanu-el. Matthew opens his book with that name for Jesus (1:23) and concludes it with Jesus' promise to be with us always: "And behold, I am with you always, until the end of the age" (28:20). Let us respond to this good news of God's coming so very close to us in Jesus with Psalms 124 and 91.

Psalms 124 and 91

Right side:
Had not the Lord been with us, let Israel say—
had not the Lord been with us—
when enemies rose up against us,
they would have swallowed us alive.

Left side:
The torrent would have swept over us,
over us would have swept the raging water.
Blessed be the Lord who did not leave us.

Right side:
We were set free like a bird from the hunter's trap.
The trap was broken and we were freed.

Left side:
To the angels God has given command about us,
that they guard us in all our ways.
On their hands they bear us up,
lest we dash our foot against a rock.

Right side:
Because you cling to me I will deliver you, says the Lord.
I will set you on high because you acknowledge my
      name.

Left side:
You will call upon me and I will answer you.
I will be with you in distress.
I will deliver and glorify you and will show you my sal-
      vation.

All:
(Repeat the opening song)
"O Come, O Come Emmanuel!"

REVIEW OF CONTENTS

Objectives: To review and reinforce, through comparison of some of the introductory texts common to Mark and Matthew, some general characteristics of Matthew's gospel; and to demonstrate how scholars use the comparison of synoptic texts to draw conclusions about the sources, pastoral concerns, and contributions of the evangelist to a particular gospel.

Time: 25 minutes

The following review exercise should be divided up among the participants. It is not, however, intended for group discussion, but for a quick review and clarification of what has been already presented by Perkins in the preparatory reading. Therefore, it would be better to divide the questions (numbers 1-4) among the participants, one quarter working on each question. It may be helpful to suggest working in twos, so that participants who feel more at ease with the material can help others. Participants who finish more quickly than others can be encouraged to work on other questions in addition to the one assigned. All participants should do question 5 in addition to one of the other questions.

Also, in the last 5-10 minutes of this activity, the leader should take up question 5 for discussion, at the same time clarifying any difficulties participants had with other questions. It should not be necessary, however, to discuss all questions in detail, if the leader circulates among the group addressing difficulties while participants work on the questions. If a gospel parallel book is available, this will facilitate the exercise.

In this exercise, you will be asked to compare some of the introductory passages of Mark's gospel with their parallels in Matthew, as suggested in Perkins, chapter 13. The final question will help you review and summarize the results of this comparison. Read the given passages from the gospels and answer the questions as directed by your leader.

1. Read both Mark's and Matthew's accounts of the ministry of John the Baptist (Mark 1:2-8 and Matthew 3:1-12).

a. Note the verses in Matthew's text that also occur in Mark's text.

b. How does Matthew "correct" Mark 1:2? What concerns of Matthew are reflected in this change? (See Perkins, p. 215.)

Mark has thrown together a saying from the prophet Malachi with the intended one from Isaiah. Matthew uses only the Isaiah text. In general, Matthew is concerned with Jesus as the fulfillment of the Old Law, and particularly, with the fulfillment of prophetic texts. His audience is Jewish-Christian and the continuity of Jesus with the past is important.

c. Read the content of John's preaching, verses 7-12 in Matthew. Does Mark include these texts? Why do scholars conclude that Matthew took these sayings from Q? (See Perkins, p. 215, par. 2.)

Mark does not include all these texts. These sayings are used also by Luke in this context. Sayings that occur in Matthew and Luke, but not in Mark, are generally attributed to Q.

Which theme of Matthew is being emphasized in the preaching of Jesus here?

The theme of judgment; notice the reference to fire and to the separation of the grain and chaff.

What is the reason for Matthew's emphasis on this theme? (See Perkins, p. 215.)

Matthew is responding to a problem with false prophets and those who think they will be saved merely by imitating Jesus' miracles. He wants to emphasize that faithfulness to Jesus' teaching is the criterion by which we will be judged.

d. Luke 3:7 says, "He would say to the crowds that came out to be baptized by him: 'You brood of vipers!' " To whom does Matthew's gospel address the same condemnation (Mt 3:7)?

Matthew directs this condemnation to the Pharisees and Sadducees. (You may wish to direct participants to a review of the significance of these groups in Perkins, pp. 32-35.)

According to Perkins, what seems to be the explanation of this difference between Luke and Matthew (p. 215)?

The polemic against the Pharisees in Matthew seems to have been motivated by the role they were playing in the Judaism of the time in which this gospel was written. After A.D. 70, the teachings of the Pharisees dominated Judaism. It seems that they emphasized detailed observance of the Law, perhaps in an effort to restore and maintain their religion and culture. Matthew will continue to emphasize that Jesus showed a way to a greater righteousness; mercy and persons come before such detailed observance. This, according to Matthew, is the correct interpretation of God's Law.

2. Read carefully the parallel texts about the baptism of Jesus: Matthew 3:13-17 and Mark 1:9-11.

a. Note the text in Matthew that is also found in Mark.

b. What are the two major changes that Matthew has made in this account of Jesus' baptism? (See Perkins, p. 215.)

First, Matthew adds the dialogue between John and Jesus to show that Jesus did not need a baptism of repentance, since he was sinless. His baptism was in fulfillment of God's plan. Second, the divine voice speaks only to Jesus in Mark, whereas in Matthew a public declaration is made. This change probably reflects the departure from the messianic secret in Mark, which does not exist in Matthew.

c. Why do you think Matthew wants to show that Jesus fulfills God's plan (vs. 14)?

For Matthew's Jewish-Christian community, it is important that they see the continuity between the Old Law and the New Law established by Jesus. Matthew emphasizes in many places that Jesus is the "fulfillment" of the promises and prophecies of the Old Testament. (See Perkins, p. 221 and the references to Matthew's use of this theme listed there.)

3. Read and compare the accounts of Jesus' testing in the wilderness in Mark 1:12-13 and Matthew 4:1-11.

a. Notice that very little of this Matthew text occurs in the account by Mark. Most of Matthew's account, however, can be found in Luke's gospel. What does this indicate about the source of the content of the temptations of Jesus? (See Perkins, p. 216.)

Materials found in both Matthew and Luke, but not in Mark are generally attributed to Q.

b. Both the tempter and Jesus use citations from the Old

94

Testament (Deuteronomy and Psalms). Since this incident occurs at the beginning of Jesus' public life, what does it reveal about how we might expect Jesus to relate to the Old Law? (See footnote to Mt 4:1-11 in NAB; also Perkins, p. 221.)

In Matthew 5:17, Jesus declares, "Do not think that I have come to destroy the Law and the prophets; I have not come to destroy but to fulfill." Jesus, as Matthew presents him, demands fidelity to the Law and the prophets, an even greater fidelity than proposed by the Pharisees. The spirit of the Law takes on greater significance. "A higher righteousness" is called for. This passage shows Jesus' obedience to God as Matthew's community understands the God of the Scriptures.

4. Read and compare the following accounts of the initiation of Jesus' preaching of the kingdom of God: Mark 1:14-15 and Matthew 4:12-17.

a. Note the presence of Mark's material in Matthew's version of the beginning of Jesus' preaching. What phrases within this material, especially in the "words of Jesus," differ between the two accounts? Suggest explanations of these differences (Perkins, p. 216).

Mark has Jesus say, "This is the time of fulfillment." Since Matthew has expanded on this theme in vs. 14-16, he does not need to include this phrase. This is an example of Matthew's greater concern with Jesus as fulfillment of prophecy and then a subsequent editorial change. Perkins notes that Matthew drops Mark's phrase "believe in the gospel" to avoid having Jesus speak like a Christian missionary. The theme of fulfillment has priority in Matthew's text.

b. What does Perkins suggest is the significance of the increased geographic region that Jesus covers and addresses here and in other parts of Matthew's gospel? (See Perkins pp. 216 and 218; the footnote to Mt 4:12-17 in NAB is also helpful.)

Perkins suggests that the additional explanation of Jesus' movements is connected to the prophecy that Matthew sees Jesus fulfilling. The NAB footnote points out that this particular prophecy refers to the restoration of the Northern Kingdom; hence, Matthew's inclusion of this area. The geographic region covered by Jesus in Matthew's gospel as a whole is increased as compared to Mark's. It may indicate the actual geographic region in which Matthew's community was located or from which they came.

5. Summary discussion questions:

a. Mark's gospel is the obvious source of some of Matthew's text, as you saw from the comparisons above. What were the other sources corresponding to the following material in Matthew:

— the material found in both Matthew and Luke, for example the content of Jesus' testing in the wilderness?

This is material from Q. For review of what the Q source is, see Perkins, p. 63.

— prophetic sayings, such as Matthew 4:15-16?

The Old Testament. Matthew uses this source more than any of the other evangelists.

— texts, such as those condemning the Pharisees (Mt 3:7), found only in Matthew?

These could be Matthew's own (or Matthew's own community's) interpretation of the tradition. They could also be from other sources, such as the Gospel of Thomas or sources unknown to us.

b. What concerns or themes of Matthew and his community have you identified from the passages above? The answer to this question should be an accumulation of answers from the four questions above.

Participants will have encountered some or all of the concerns in the passages used. Concerns and themes reflected overall are themes of fulfillment and/or continuity of the Old Law, judgment, Jesus as true interpreter of the Law (as opposed to the Pharisees and Sadducees), polemic against the Pharisees, and increased geographic relevance of Jesus.

VIDEO

Objectives: To focus on Matthew's concern to reconcile Gentile and Jewish Christianity, the old with the new; and to reflect on the unique elements of his gospel which enable him to accomplish this.

Time: 20 minutes

Matthew: The Wise Scribe

As you view this video, please make note of the following:

1. What was the position of each of these persons or groups concerning the place of the Gentiles within the church?

Judaizers _____

Paul _____

Peter and James _____

2. What was Matthew's main concern in writing his gospel?

_____

Video Outline

Matthew: The Wise Scribe

1. Crisis in the church
   a. Situation today
   b. Situation in the early church: Gentile and Jewish Christians
   c. Attitudes toward Gentiles and the Law:
      Judaizers, Paul, and James

2. Antioch: source of Matthew's gospel and eye of the storm
   a. Gentile mission in Antioch
   b. Problem with Judaizers
   c. Confrontation between Peter and Paul

3. The Gospel of Matthew
   a. Situation in Antioch: in search of a synthesis
   b. Loss of authority:
      destruction of the temple and Jerusalem
      deaths of Peter, James, and Paul
      break with the synagogue
   c. Matthew's synthesis: preserve the old in light of the new
   d. Authority rooted in the teaching and person of Jesus
   e. Ecclesial nature of the gospel

BREAK

(10 minutes)

LEARNING ACTIVITY

Objective: To enable participants to become more familiar with Matthew's gospel, especially with the sayings of Jesus as he organizes them into sermons. To further explore the relationship between how Jesus is presented and the needs of a particular community. To lay a firmer basis for reflection on the gospel as a guide to their own Christian discipleship.

Time: 25 minutes

Using whatever technique you have found to work in the organization of small groups, ask the participants to form five groups of five or less and assign each group one of the five sermons of Jesus as indicated below. Make sure all the sermons are covered, even if this means creating smaller groups. Since the sermons were part of the preparatory reading, it should not be necessary for each group to read the assigned text in its entirety. Each question indicates the verses being specifically referred to in the text. In that way, there should be about 10 minutes left for summary and discussion after the groups have accomplished their task.

In the final summary and discussion, it is not necessary to go over in detail each of the questions assigned to the groups. Questions have been provided for the leader as a guide in drawing together and further reflecting on the research for the whole group. These questions are not in the Workbook. After each of the final questions, the group numbers and research question numbers to which the summary question best refers is indicated.

In this activity, you will be asked by your leader to study and discuss one of the five sermons of Jesus presented in Matthew's gospel. This will be done in a group, according to your leader's directions. Questions are provided to aid your investigation of each sermon. At the end of the activity, your group will be asked to share with all the participants some of the reflections on the questions you have discussed. Make notes in the space provided to aid your memory and discussion.

Group 1

The Sermon on the Mount, Matthew 5:1-7:29.

1. How do you picture this sermon taking place? (Describe the setting, vs. 1-2.)

Jesus is up on the mountainside away from the crowds. His disciples gather around him.

2. Summarize Jesus' sayings about the following issues in this sermon:

a. relationship of Christ and his kingdom to the Old Law (5:17-19)

Jesus did not come to abolish the Old Law, but to fulfill it. He admonishes those who would break the Law and lead others to do the same. He offers a reward to those who would obey the Law. The latter shall enter the kingdom of God. The remainder of the sermon actually calls on the disciples of Jesus to go beyond the literal obedience of the Law to obeying even its spirit.

b. rifts between members of the community (5:22, 23-25; 7:1-5; 7:12)

Jesus admonishes those who would express anger and abusive language against their brothers and sisters, counsels community members to settle misunderstandings with others in the community before approaching the altar, warns against judging others and ignoring our own failures, and pronounces the golden rule, "Treat others the way you would have them treat you," as a summary of the whole Law and the prophets.

c. relationship to outsiders (5:43-48)

This is an example of Jesus' call to his followers to live the Law even more perfectly. Disciples of Jesus must love their enemies as well as their own brothers and sisters and national group. They must return kindness for hostility and persecution. The Law is presented here as a perfection to strive toward, rather than as the minimum requirement of discipleship.

3. How are Jesus' followers to distinguish between a true prophet and a false one, a true disciple and a false one (7:15-23)?

The "true" are distinguished from the "false" by their good deeds, their obedience to the will of God (vs. 21). Empty words and miraculous powers do not win the kingdom of God.

4. Matthew 7:24-27 contrasts two types of foundations on which Jesus' followers can build their lives. To what does he compare these foundations? Using the information you gathered in questions 1-3 above, summarize briefly what this sermon presents as a firm foundation for the true disciple of Jesus.

The foundations are compared to rock or sand as foundations for a house. Answers may vary, but should include some or all of the following: kindness and forgiveness toward other members of our communities, hospitality toward outsiders, an attitude of reconciliation even toward those who harm us, attentiveness and obedience to the will of God expressed in the words of Jesus, and the evidence of good deeds to support our beliefs.

Group 2

The Disciple on Mission to Israel, Matthew 9:35-11:1.

1. What kind of person does Matthew show Jesus to be at the beginning of this sermon (9:35-38)? To whom is the sermon addressed (10:1-4)? To whom are the apostles being sent (10:5-6)?

Jesus is a person moved by compassion for those who suffer. The sermon is addressed to the twelve apostles. The apostles are being sent to "the lost sheep of the house of Israel," in other words, to Jews who did not come to believe in Jesus, or, as indicated in 9:35-38, to those who seem to be cast out from the main society because of disease or other reasons.

2. In your own words, describe the message and ministry the apostles are to bring to the people, as presented in the following texts:
a. 10:7-8
b. 10:27
c. 10:37-39

a. Use their gift of healing to restore those for whom Jesus had been moved to compassion.

b. Speak the message of the kingdom of God as Jesus had revealed it to them.

c. Teach and show the urgency of Jesus' mission. The disciples are to give first priority to this mission and be willing to suffer for it. In doing so, unselfishly, they will discover who they truly are.

3. How are the apostles to conduct themselves? (Check 10:9-10, 10:11-14, 10:17-20.)

Not be concerned with their material welfare, be dependent on those they serve; be practical in seeking hospitality, stay where they are welcome but leave if they are not; be wise in trusting others, since they could be betrayed and persecuted on account of Jesus. (This was already the experience of the Christian community.)

What practical concern lies behind the promise of a reward for those who welcome Jesus' disciples, as in 10:40-42? (See Perkins, p. 220.)

In the experience of Matthew and his community, wandering teachers and missionaries are often mistreated. Here Jesus speaks of a reward as an encouragement to those would be hospitable to his disciples, even if they are not believers (implied). This will count on the day of judgment.

4. Jesus speaks words of encouragement to his apostles. Summarize the sources of hope Jesus offers to those who undertake this mission in his name. (See especially the following verses in chapter 10:15, 20, 30-33, 38-39, 40-42.)

Jesus threatens retribution for those who do not welcome the disciples; the Spirit of God will be with them during persecution to strengthen and enlighten them; God will care for them even more than he evidently does for his creation (flock of sparrows); each of them is important to the Father; Jesus will acknowledge them before his Father; the disciple who suffers on account of Jesus and his mission will discover his true identity; finally, those who are hospitable to the disciples will be justly rewarded.

Group 3

The Parables of the Kingdom, Matthew 13:1-53.

1. Describe the setting, the location, and the audience for this sermon of Jesus (13:1-2).

The sermon is delivered from a boat in a lake to a "great crowd" that has gathered on the lake shore.

2. Recall that in Mark's gospel the disciples of Jesus generally responded in fear and misunderstanding to the teachings of Jesus. How do the disciples in Matthew's gospel compare? (Check 13:11, 16, 51.)

In Matthew's gospel, Jesus gives his disciples special knowledge "of the mysteries of the reign of God" that he does not give to all. Furthermore, the disciples truly "see" and "hear" the message intended by Christ. They are not the blind disciples as Mark presents them. They profess this understanding (vs. 51).

3. What does Jesus ask of his disciples in Matthew's presentation of the parables of the treasure and the pearl (vs. 44-46)?

These parables show the priority that must be placed on being members of the kingdom. The disciples are asked to put all their efforts into the real treasure—the kingdom of God.

What do the parables of the mustard seed and the leaven (vs. 31-33) tell us about how the reign of God grows in this world?

These parables reveal the nature of the kingdom; it does not come about by some overwhelming display or revolution, but gradually. It grows from a very small and seemingly insignificant beginning to something great and obvious (like the mustard tree), and invades the whole world (as the yeast does the flour).

4. According to Jesus' parables presented in this sermon, what is the difference between the reign of God as it ex-

ists in this world now and the final reign of God as it will exist at the end of the world? (Check vs. 29-30, 37-43, 47-50.)

Now, the kingdom of God exists in the ambiguity of this world; good and evil exist together. In fact, it is often not possible to distinguish the two. But at the end of time, the day of judgment, the two will be separated and the good will triumph. This is the ultimate fulfillment of the kingdom intended by Jesus.

Why might this teaching of Jesus about the distinction between the kingdom now and the kingdom yet to come be significant and helpful to Matthew's community?

Apparently, Matthew's community was struggling with the question of how the reign of God could be established if evil and hardship were still so evident. Where was the perfect peace and harmony prophesied by Isaiah and the other prophets? How could this be the messiah? As a result, many grew cold, discouraged and indifferent. Matthew's gospel addresses this reality, and tries to clarify through the teachings of Jesus, and of the prophets whom he quotes, that the present situation was to be expected. Such is the nature of the kingdom in this world.

Group 4

Relationships within the Community, Matthew 18:1-35.

1. What prompts Jesus to give this sermon? How does the sermon begin? To whom is it addressed (vs. 1, 21)?

Jesus begins the sermon in response to a question from the disciples about who will be the greatest in his kingdom. He continues when Peter raises a question about how often one is expected to forgive another.

2. What does Jesus' reference to children in this sermon (vs. 12-14) tell us about what it means to be a disciple? (See Perkins, p. 225.)

In Matthew's account of this incident, Jesus asks not only that one "receive the kingdom" as a child would, but that the disciple become like a child, humble and insignificant (in those days).

3. What kind of problems within this early Christian community does Matthew seem to address in the following verses of this sermon:
a. 6-7
b. 15-16
c. 21-35

a. leading "little ones" astray through false teaching and giving scandal

b. rivalries and misunderstandings among members of the community and of the same family, perhaps, as well as failure to deal adequately with this problem

c. failure to forgive one another, or the setting of limits on one's forgiveness

4. Recall that Jesus is addressing his disciples, the leaders of the community here. Peter, for example, is present (vs. 21). What message is Jesus giving them in vs. 12-14?

Jesus is emphasizing the importance of each person in his Father's kingdom. The disciples are to give special attention to those "who have wandered off," the little ones who have become lost. It is not sufficient to pay attention only to those who already believe.

5. Matthew also offers words of comfort and hope to his community in this sermon of Jesus. Summarize the message presented in verses 18 and 19-20.

Jesus expresses his confidence in the power of the community to interpret his message and mission (v. 18). He also promises to be present and hear their prayers, even where just two or three are gathered in his name.

Group 5

The End of the World and Judgment, Matthew 24:1-25:46.

1. To whom is Jesus speaking in this sermon? Where is he and when does it take place (24:1-4, 26:1-2)?

Jesus is speaking to his disciples who have come to him privately. He has just left the temple precincts and is seated on the Mount of Olives. It is just two days before Passover and the beginning of his Passion.

2. Matthew's community is confused by the continued presence of evil after the reign of God has already been initiated by Jesus. Briefly state how this problem is addressed in the following verses from this text.
a. 24:11-14
b. 24:30-35
c. 24:44-51
d. 25:1-13

a. The presence of false prophets is recognized as something expected to occur before the second coming of Jesus. The increase of evil and the consequent disillusionment of Jesus' followers is acknowledged. The disciples are encouraged to be faithful to the end; those who do so will be rewarded. They will witness the spread of the kingdom to the whole world.

b. The disciples are assured that the Son of Man will indeed return. Signs are already present to those who would read them. That time will be soon. They are also reminded of the words of Jesus that will endure forever.

c. Jesus speaks of the necessity for continued attentiveness and vigilance. The disciple who wishes to be a part of the kingdom of God cannot give up, become lax, or give in to despair. He/she must be in constant readiness, working for the kingdom, when the Son of Man returns.

d. This is another warning to those who would "grow cold." The disciples must be in constant readiness, alert to the arrival of the bridegroom.

3. In chapter 25, those who will be saved are contrasted with those who will not through three sets of images. What does each of the following sets of images tell us about what it means to be a true disciple of Jesus:

a. wise virgins and foolish virgins

a. True disciples are in constant readiness for the kingdom; they do not grow weary in waiting for the Lord's return.

b. servants who invested their silver pieces and servants who buried their silver pieces

b. True disciples use their gifts in the service of the kingdom. They recognize that is why they have received those gifts, so they courageously invest them, despite the risk that they may fail. The disciples will be called upon to account for these gifts. Gifts are not intended to be guarded selfishly or buried out of fear, but to be put to use on behalf of God's kingdom.

c. the sheep and the goats

c. The contrast set up by this set of images is not intrinsically related to sheep and goats except insofar as they are separated by the shepherd. On the last day, the true disciples will be shown to be those who have served the needs of the poor and suffering—the little ones for whom Jesus showed compassion.

Summary questions to guide sharing of above research:

1. Who was important in Jesus' kingdom? (Group 2:1, 3. Group 4:2, 3. Group 5:3c.)

Whereas all are welcome in Jesus' kingdom, special mention is made of the "little ones," those who would humble themselves to become like children, the lost ones, those like sheep without a shepherd, the sick and suffering, those who give all in the service of the kingdom, and those who are attentive to "the little ones."

2. What kind of pastoral concerns did Matthew confront using the sayings of Jesus? (Group 1:2. Group 2:3. Group 3:4. Group 5:2.)

Discouragement and despondency at the presence of evil, disagreements and feuding among the members, perhaps the presence of non-Jews and the difficulty of knowing how they should be treated, and the question of identity of the community, i.e. the relationship between being Jewish and being Christian.

3. For Matthew, what characterizes the true disciple? (Group 1:3, 4. Group 3:2. Group 4:2. Group 5:3).

The emphasis in the sermons was on faithfulness to the teaching of Jesus; steadfastness in the face of difficulties; humility and willingness to suffer for the kingdom; true charity, especially to those in need; watchfulness and attentiveness, which imply a whole life dedicated to discipleship; unfailing belief in the return of the Son of Man and the fulfillment of the kingdom; obedience to the Law that aims at perfection (obeying its spirit); and a willingness to give all for the sake of the kingdom.

FAITH SHARING

Objective: To encourage participants to reflect on the relevance of Matthew's gospel and the particular features of that gospel to their experience of Christian community today.

Time: 25 minutes

This exercise should combine reflection and sharing. Most of the participants will have already thought about these questions, since they flow naturally out of the other activities of the session. Allow five minutes for individuals to organize their thoughts and make notes on the following questions. Depending on the size of the group, invite them to share their reflections within small groups or with the whole group.

1. Reflect back on your own reading and research in Matthew's gospel as well as that learned from the video presentation. Are the concerns of Matthew and his community very similar, somewhat similar, or totally different from those you experience in your present Christian community? Explain.

Answers will vary. Some participants may have difficult experiences around work in parishes, etc., that could come up here. Be sensitive, but try to move the group to seeing that the frustration for Matthew's community and perhaps for many today is in seeing, through the eyes of faith, the presence of the kingdom amidst human frailty.

2. Are Matthew's words of warning regarding how we are to be judged relevant to Christians today? Why or why not?

Discussion here will probably focus on world poverty, as well as local problems, and the question of how to respond as Christians. Sometimes a sense of despair and paralyzing guilt can result from an awareness of the overwhelming nature of such problems as world poverty. On the other hand, complete indifference is also not a Christian response. Note the practical nature of Matthew's approach to problems. We are accountable before God, according to Matthew's gospel, for how we treat the "least" among us; we are also called upon to rely on the presence of Jesus and to use whatever gifts we are given in the service of the kingdom.

3. Which words of comfort and hope in Matthew's gospel did you find especially helpful to your situation in Christian community today (your family, friends, parish)? How so?

Answers will be personal.

CLOSING PRAYER

Time: 10 minutes

Preparation:
Settle the group into a prayerful mode by playing a piece of classical music for about one minute; then turn it down, but let it play as background to the Call to Remember. During this quieting, relight the candle, or start a new stick of incense, if you are using it.

A Call to Remember

Leader:
The reign of God did not seem to produce perfection. Should not the messiah have brought total peace and happiness? Many became discouraged; their faith grew cold. Matthew encourages his community to trust in the power of Jesus and his continued presence. He shows how ambiguities will continue to exist while the reign of God is in this world.

(Listen for about two minutes to some classical music.)

Leader:
Matthew applied the words of his sacred books, the Jewish Scriptures, to Jesus' life and to Matthew's own community. For example, the words of the prophet Hosea (6:6) must have been precious to him, for he has Jesus repeat them in chapter 12, verse 7. Here is the context for Matthew's first quoting Hosea:

> *Reader:*
> A reading from the gospel according to Matthew (9:9-13):

> *All:*
> Glory to you, O Lord.

Reader:
As Jesus passed on from there, he saw a man named Matthew sitting at his customs table. Jesus said to him, "Follow me." Matthew got up and followed him. While he was at the table in Matthew's house, many tax collectors and sinners came in and sat with Jesus and his disciples. The Pharisees saw this and said to the disciples: "Why does your teacher eat with tax collectors and sinners?" Jesus overheard this and said, "Those who are well do not need a doctor, but those who are sick do. Go and learn the meaning of the words (from Hosea): 'I desire mercy, not sacrifice.' I did not come to call the righteous but sinners."

> *Reader:*
> This is the gospel of the Lord.

All:
Praise to you, Lord Jesus Christ!

A Call to Respond

Leader:
"I desire mercy, not sacrifice," must have been important to Matthew and his community, perhaps flowing from his personal experience of having been so accepted and welcomed by the merciful Jesus. What gospel words are particularly important to you, words which you apply to your life, your family, parish, world? What is good news for you? Please share those words of good news with the person next to you.

(Allow two minutes of sharing.)

Leader:
Let us pray:

(Pause)
Your words are spirit and life. Thank you for staying with us, Lord Jesus, through your word in Scripture and through the good news which we speak and are for one another. We join you in your prayer as you stand before the face of God.

(The leader then stands and extends his or her hands with the palms facing upward.)

Let us stand, and in the Jewish manner of prayer, lift our hands to God in supplication as we pray:

All:
Our Father and Mother, who art in heaven . . .
for the kingdom, the power and the glory are yours, now and forever. Amen.

Concluding Song
O Come, O Come, Emmanuel!

FOLLOW-UP

A. Journaling

Matthew presents Jesus as a great teacher. Jesus' words to his disciples and followers are very important in guiding their lives. His words reveal the will of God and the true meaning of God's law. Recall sayings of Jesus that are either particularly appealing to you, helpful in your life, or disturbing to you. You may want to leaf through Matthew's gospel to refresh your memory or discover sayings you were not aware of. Make a list of several sayings for each category. You may also wish to add other categories. Reflect on and write about the significance of one or two of these sayings in your life.

B. Additional Resources

1. Read as much as possible of the gospel of Matthew using the outline of the gospel in Perkins, p. 219.

2. If your Bible has an introduction to the gospel of Matthew, read it.

3. Read: Anthony Marinelli, *Understanding the Gospels* Chapter 4, "The Synoptic Gospels," pp. 60-67.

4. Read: *The Catholic Study Bible,* "Matthew," RG 388-405.

5. Scholars believe that Matthew's community was in Antioch in Syria. Using the Hammond *Atlas of the Bible Lands,* locate Antioch.

C. Further Reading

The New Jerome Biblical Commentary, "Matthew," Article 42.

Philip A. Cunningham, *Jesus and the Evangelists,* "The Matthean Jesus: Wisdom of God Incarnate," pp. 46-78.

John F. O'Grady, *The Four Gospels and the Jesus Tradition,* "The Jesus Tradition and the Church: Matthew," pp. 155-212.

8. Luke: Jesus the Lord

Preparation

- Read Perkins, Chapter 14, "Luke: Jesus the Lord."
- Read Luke 9:51-19:27.
- Reflect on the FOCUS statement and the REVIEW OF CONTENTS questions.

General Goals

To help participants gain an overview of the Gospel of Luke; to focus on the journey to Jerusalem section and the lessons that Jesus teaches about the nature and demands of discipleship in that section; to gain a personal appreciation of the nature of prayer as Luke presents it.

FOCUS

In the Gospel of Luke the ministry of Jesus is divided into three sections: his ministry in Galilee; his journey to Jerusalem; and his ministry in Jerusalem. Luke's journey narrative has three sections: 9:51-13:21; 13:22-17:10; and 17:11-19:27. The opening verse of each of these divisions states that Jesus was on his way to Jerusalem. "On the way" there are those who will accept Jesus and there are those who will reject him. Luke understands discipleship as a call to follow Jesus and the true disciple is the one who hears the word of God and keeps it (8:19-21). Luke's model of the "first disciple" is Mary, an example of faithfulness and wholehearted response to God's initiative. The disciples must leave all things to follow Jesus and to walk along the way that Jesus has set out for them.

OPENING PRAYER

Time: 5 minutes

Preparation
Prepare a simple centerpiece of a single candle. Leave it unlit as the group gathers.

Leader:
We have come full circle, as we conclude our sessions together. We opened eight sessions ago with a candle, and tonight, so much more aware and enlightened about Scripture and its meanings for us, we give thanks for the light of Christ, whom we celebrate tonight with Luke and his community. Let us hear the word and respond.

> *Reader:*
> A reading from the prophet Isaiah (58:6-11) . . .

The biblical text should be read from the Bible.

When the reader says, "Then your light shall break forth like the dawn," the leader lights the candle in the center of the group.

> *Reader:*
> This is the word of the Lord.

> *All:*
> Thanks be to God.

Psalm 146

Right side:
Bless the Lord, my whole life!
I will praise the Lord all my life;
I will sing praise to my God while I live.

Left side:
Happy are we whose help is God,
whose hope is in the Lord,
our God who is faithful forever,
securing justice for the oppressed,
giving food to the hungry.

Right side:
The Lord sets captives free,
the Lord gives sight to the blind.
The Lord raises up those who were bent over.

Left side:
The Lord protects strangers;
the orphans and the widows God sustains,
but the way of the wicked God thwarts.

All:
Our God shall reign forever,
our Lord for all generations. Alleluia!

Reader:
A reading from the holy gospel according to Luke
(4:14-21).

All:
Glory to you, O Lord.

The gospel text should be read from the Scriptures.

Reader:
This is the good news of the Lord.

All:
Praise to you, Lord Jesus Christ.

Leader:
Let us pray.

All:

Let your light, Lord Jesus, break forth in us like a dawn,
heal our wounds and open our eyes so that we may
know you and the power of your Spirit. We ask this in
your name. Amen.

The leader extinguishes the candle.

REVIEW OF CONTENTS

Objective: To insure that the participants have a broad overview of Luke's gospel.

Time: 25 minutes

Ask the participants to choose the phrase that most adequately completes the sentences below. Remind them that this is simply a discussion starter and a way of review. It is not a test. Moreover, there may well be more than one correct answer.

When they have completed the task, ask them to compare their answers in small groups for about five minutes. In the large group, quickly go down the page and comment on the correct answers. If anyone questions an answer, ask the person for his or her reasons, and then have the person explain the response he or she chose. As much as possible, let others in the group respond to the questioner.

Check the phrase(s) that most adequately completes the sentence:

1. According to the preface (vs.1-4), the main purpose of Luke's Gospel is:

      to instruct Theophilus about the practical implications of being a Christian;

      to write a history of Jesus and the first disciples;

X   to assure his readers that what the church preaches goes back to the preaching of Jesus and the earliest disciples.

2. The gospel of Luke incorporates much of the material that is found in Mark, and:

X   adds passages from Q;

X   includes sections that are unique to Luke;

      uses the imagery from John's gospel.

3. Three major additions that Luke makes to Mark's gospel are: 1. most of the instructions given to the church on the journey to Jerusalem (9:51-19:27); 2. accounts of the resurrection appearances (24); and 3:

      the call of the twelve apostles (6:12-16);

X   account of Jesus' birth and early life (1:5-2:40);

      story of the temptation in the desert (4:1-13).

4. Luke divides the ministry of Jesus into 1. his Galilean ministry; 2. journey to Jerusalem; and 3. his ministry in Jerusalem. One of the common themes that binds these episodes together is:

X the contrast of those who accept Jesus with those
who reject him;
blocks of teaching organized into identifiable
sermons;
the image of journey.

5. Jesus tells the parables of the lost sheep, the woman
searching for a lost coin and the prodigal son (15:1-32) in
order to:
teach that one must have care and concern for
others;
X give examples of God's love and mercy;
X say that Christians ought to celebrate and rejoice.

6. The parables of the lost sheep, coin and prodigal son
focus on the basic issue between Jesus and the Lukan
Pharisees:
X No one is outside the circle of God's love;
X Salvation is offered even to the sinners and outcasts
of society;
X Being religious involves more than the keeping of
laws and regulations.

7. Jesus' opening sermon in Luke (4:16-30) proclaims that
the Scripture's promise of a time of salvation is fulfilled in
Jesus. Some signs of a new age of salvation are:
X repentance and celebrations of joy which are
responses to Jesus' preaching;
X persons who praise and glorify God like Mary and
Zechariah who bless God;
the fall of the Roman empire.

8. In the threefold division of the gospel, Luke presents a
pattern of salvation history. The first period is God's
promises to Israel which includes those who wait for the
coming of the Lord like Simeon and Anna and culminates
in John the Baptist. The second period is Jesus' ministry.
The third period is:
Jesus' death and resurrection;
the second coming of Christ;
X the church's mission.

9. Luke presents Jesus as the universal savior. This univer-
salism manifests itself in the inclusion of non-Jews in
Christianity and in:
X the inclusion of the poor, the outcasts, women, and
sinners;
evangelizing the Emperor Augustus;
letting the Samaritans pray in the synagogue.

VIDEO

Objective: To help participants come to appreciate the journey section of Luke's gospel as an expression of Luke's characteristic concerns and his teaching about discipleship.

Time: 20 minutes

Jesus' Journey to Jerusalem

As you view this video, please make note of the following:

1. What are the three stages of salvation history outlined by Luke?

a. _____

b. _____

c. _____

2. What are the qualities of a disciple which Luke outlines in his journey section?

a. _____

b. _____

c. _____

d. _____

e. _____

f. _____

Video Outline

Jesus' Journey to Jerusalem

1. Luke divides salvation history into three phases
   a. history of Israel
   b. the ministry of Jesus (Luke's gospel)
   c. the age of the church and the Holy Spirit (Acts)

2. Jesus' journey to Jerusalem is the centerpiece of Luke's gospel
   a. Luke provides little detail of the journey
   b. Jesus going up to Jerusalem illustrates his own obedience and acceptance of the cross

3. The journey as a lesson about the nature of discipleship
   a. A disciple listens to the word
      Mary, the Mother of Jesus
      Martha and Mary
   b. A disciple loves without limit
      The Parable of the Good Samaritan
   c. A disciple is rooted in prayer
   d. A disciple is committed to the kingdom
      The Parable of the Tower
   e. A disciple is dependent on God
      Jesus' sayings about wealth
   f. A disciple is compassionate
      Jesus' ministry to the marginalized
      Jesus' critique of the Pharisees

BREAK

(10 minutes)

LEARNING ACTIVITY

Objective: To provide participants with an overview of the Lukan episodes which contrast those who accept Jesus with those who reject him.

Time: 25 minutes

Prepare the group for this exercise by reviewing with them the Lukan theme of the acceptance or rejection of Jesus. Then assign each of the passages found in the workbook to one or more persons or groups.

Read the passage below which is assigned to you by your Program Leader. Make note of the character(s) who either accept or reject Jesus and how they are contrasted in the story.

Luke 2:25-38

Luke 4:16-30

Luke 7:36-50

Luke 9:51-54 and 17:11-19

Luke 23:39-43

In the passage you read, which characters or groups accept Jesus? Which reject him? How are they contrasted in the passage(s)?

Luke 2:25-38—Simeon prophesies that Jesus will be a sign of contradiction. Anna receives him with joy and becomes a witness to the Lord.

Luke 4:16-30—The group in the synagogue in Nazareth is contrasted to those who were instructed in Galilee.

Luke 7:36-50—The sinful woman is contrasted to Simon the Pharisee.

Luke 9:51-54 and 17:11-19—The rejection of the Samaritans and the return of the Samaritan leper who gave thanks.

Luke 23:39-43—Two criminals are crucified with Jesus. One shares the mockery of the crowd, challenging Jesus' claim to be savior, the other acknowledges his own sinfulness and Jesus' innocence.

> What lesson is Luke teaching through these episodes of acceptance and rejection?

Luke uses the theme of acceptance and rejection throughout Jesus' ministry to provide an explanation of the eventual rejection of Jesus. He is seeking to demonstrate that the rejection of Jesus is rooted not in the truth of the charges against him, but in the attitudes of the religious leaders. They were unable to recognize Jesus' ministry of reconciliation to the lost, nor could they celebrate with him their return as a sign of God's salvation.

FAITH SHARING

Objective: To reflect on the meaning of prayer in the gospel of Luke and the importance of prayer in our own lives.

Time: 25 minutes

Prayer was the primary way in which Jesus deepened his relationship with God. Throughout his gospel, Luke indicates how important prayer is in the life of Jesus. In every decisive moment of his life he is at prayer: after his baptism (3:21), at the beginning of his ministry (4:16), before choosing the twelve (6:12), in the synagogue (4:16), and on the mountain top (9:28). Luke gives examples of prayer in the Our Father (11:2-4), in the Canticles of Mary (1:46-55), Zechariah (68-79) and Simeon (2:29-32). The disciples are admonished to pray always (18:1) and are assured that their prayer will not go unheard (11:5-13).

Read Luke 18:1-8.

1. The widow is described as persistent and demanding of her rights under the law. Why is she so disturbing to the judge?

Her persistence in demanding her rights is a critique of his failure to defend the powerless which is his duty. Her persistence is harmful to him because it draws public attention to his corrupt ways and discredits him.

2. Why would Jesus use a corrupt judge as an example of the power of prayer?

Perhaps for emphasis. If the persistent pleading of the widow overcomes the corrupt judge, how much more will the persistent praying of the Christian disciples attain? Unlike the judge, God is not withdrawn. Rather, God is like the father in the parable of the Prodigal Son who seeks out the lost. If an unjust judge gives in, how much more will a loving and gracious God?

3. What are some of the lessons of this parable for your own life?

The parable calls Christians to remain steadfast and persevere in prayer. Another possible interpretation is that prayer impels us to action in the way it did the widow.

4. Can you give any examples of times in which prayer has had power in your life?

CLOSING PRAYER

Time: 10 minutes

Preparation
Play some quieting classical music for a moment.

Luke's Prayers of Praise

Leader:
"Prayer was the primary way in which Jesus deepened his relationship with God." Luke, in his two opening chapters, offers us three prayers which have been used as parts of the Divine Office. In Latin they were called the *Benedictus,* put on the lips of Zechariah and used at morning prayer; Mary's *Magnificat,* used at Vespers in the evening; and Simeon's *Nunc Dimittis,* a part of Compline, the last prayer of the day.

I will pray parts of the Benedictus, we will pray the Magnificat antiphonally, and pray the Nunc Dimittis together.

Leader:
Let us pray.

(Pause)
"Blessed are you, God of Israel,
for you have visited and redeemed your people . . .
that we might serve you without fear,
in holiness and justice all the days of our lives."

(Pause)

Like John the Baptist, it is we who also "go to prepare God's ways, to give knowledge of salvation to God's people in the forgiveness of their sins, through the tender mercy of our God, when the day shall dawn upon us from on high."

(Pause. Light the candle again.)

"To give light to those who sit in darkness
and the shadow of death,
To guide our feet in the way of peace."

(Pause)
Let us respond, using Mary's song.

All:
My heart proclaims your greatness, O my God,
And my spirit rejoices in you, my Savior!

Right side:
For you have looked on your servant tenderly.
You have blessed me, poor and a serving woman.

Left side:
From this day on, all generations will call me blessed.
For you, who are mighty, have done great things for me,
and holy is your name.

Right side:
Your mercy is from generation to generation
toward those who revere you.

Left side:
You have showed strength with your arm
and scattered the proud in their grandiosity.

Right side:
You have put down the mighty from their thrones
and lifted up the lowly and powerless.

Left side:
You have filled the hungry with good things
and the rich you have sent away empty.

Right side:
You, remembering your mercy, have helped your people
as you promised our ancestors, Abraham and Sarah:
Mercy to their children forever.

All:
My heart proclaims your greatness, O my God,
And my spirit rejoices in you, my Savior!

Leader:
We have joined in Mary's song of praise. Let us join Jesus
now as he prays for us and with us and within us:

All:
Our Father and Mother . . .
for the kingdom, the power and the glory are yours, now
and forever. Amen.

(Pause)

Leader:
For our dismissal this evening, we will pray Simeon's words, so often translated: Now Lord, you may dismiss your servant in peace. After we pray

this prayer which calls Jesus a light of revelation, our light, we will exchange a kiss of peace, a blessing on each one of us. Let us pray together:

All:

Now Lord, you may let your servant go in peace,

according to your word, for my eyes have seen your salvation which you have prepared in the sight of all the
nations,

a light of revelation to the Gentiles

and the glory of your people, Israel.

Leader:

Let us exchange a gesture of peace and then go forth to
serve the Lord.

A closing song may not be necessary, as goodbyes are said.

FOLLOW-UP

A. Journaling

One of the main themes of Luke's gospel is the idea of being "on the way." Luke has marked out three stages in Jesus' journey. Each of these stages included acceptance and rejection, the valleys and the mountain tops, the decision and indecision of the crossroad—and always a firm resolve to "proceed toward Jerusalem" (9:51). In looking at your own life journey in terms of major stages, describe where you have been and where you are going. Who is with you on your journey? What experiences have taken you in different directions? Do you have a place where you can rest and pray? Have you reached out to others on the way? When have you been able to recognize the presence of Jesus "on the way?"

B. Additional Resources

1. Read as much of the gospel of Luke as you can, using the outline in Perkins, p. 232 as a guide.

2. If your Bible has an introduction to the gospel of Luke, read it.

3. Read: Anthony Marinelli, *Understanding the Gospels,* Chapter 4, "The Synoptic Gospels," pp.67-70.

4. Read: *The Catholic Study Bible,* "Luke," RG 417-437.

5. In his gospel Luke traces the spread of the gospel from Galilee to Jerusalem; in the Acts of the Apostles, he shows how the gospel spread all the way to Rome. Using the Hammond *Atlas of the Bible Lands,* find these places. Look also at Paul's missionary travels which we will study in the next semester.

C. Further Reading

The New Jerome Biblical Commentary, "Luke," Article 43.

Philip A. Cunningham, *Jesus and the Evangelists,* "The Lukan Jesus: Healing Savior," pp. 79-113.

John F. O'Grady, *The Four Gospels and the Jesus Tradition,* "The Jesus Tradition and Mercy: Luke," pp. 213-264.